Trigger Warning

Also by Brooks Eason

Travels with Bobby
Hiking in the Mountains of the American West

Fortunate Son
The Story of Baby Boy Francis

Bedtime with Buster
Conversations with a Handsome Hound

Redemption
The Two Lives of Harry Brooks

The Scoutmaster
Lessons in Service and Leadership from an American Hero

TRIGGER WARNING

TALES FROM A LIFE IN THE LAW

Brooks Eason

WordCrafts Press

Trigger Warning is memoir. It reflects the author's present recollections of experiences over time. Some names and characteristics have been changed.

Tigger Warning
Copyright © 2024
Brooks Eason

ISBN: 978-1-962218-44-3

Cover illustration by Robert Fugate. Used by permission, all rights reserved. Robert's artwork is available at robert-fugate.pixels.com.

Published by WordCrafts Press
Cody, Wyoming 82414
www.wordcrafts.net

For all my friends who gave me a rewarding life in the law.

Prologue

I sat down on our screened porch and typed the first words of this book in May 2023, two months before my sixty-sixth birthday. After practicing law for four decades, I was thinking I might be retired, but I wasn't sure.

Discerning readers might wonder how that could be. How could a man with a post-graduate degree and a lifetime of experience not know if he's retired? But it was complicated. I still had an office and a title, senior counsel at Watkins & Eager, the law firm in Jackson, Mississippi, where I "worked," and I remained on call for my biggest and best client, Ingalls Shipbuilding on the Mississippi Gulf Coast. But the phone hadn't rung in a while, I hardly ever went to the office, and I hadn't billed a single minute all year.

But I wasn't idle, at least not 24/7. I walked four miles every morning with my dog Junior, and I had just completed the manuscript for what would be my fifth book, *The Scoutmaster*, a biography of my extraordinary father. While I waited for my publisher to turn the manuscript into a book, I decided to start writing what I hoped would become my sixth book. If you're reading this, it did.

As an aside, Junior became Junior because his name was Brooks in the shelter from which we adopted him. I'd never heard of a dog named Brooks and decided adopting him was a must. But changing his name was also a must. If my beautiful wife Carrie had ever said, "Come over here, Brooks, let me give you some loving," it would have broken my heart to get my hopes up only to realize she was talking to the dog.

In the five months between May and October, Junior and I kept walking, and I kept writing, but I still did no legal work. The odds that I might be retired continued to rise. Then, a week before Halloween, I received an email that forced me to fish or cut bait.

The email was from a woman at the Mississippi Bar Association and noted that I hadn't paid my membership dues for the 2023–24 fiscal year. It was true; I hadn't. The envelope containing the bill for my dues lay unopened on the desk in my office because I hadn't been there in three months. The email further stated that I had only a week left to pony up. If I missed the deadline, I would be suspended from the practice of law, and all the courts in the state would be notified that I could no longer appear before them.

I had two immediate thoughts. First, for the Bar to suspend me and notify every court in Mississippi that I'd been given the boot would be no way to end my career. Second, two could play this game. They couldn't fire me; I would quit.

I responded to the email, said I was retired, and asked the woman to accept my email as notice of my resignation from the Bar. She said I could do that, but I might want to consider becoming an inactive member instead. It would cost me fifty dollars a year, but if I ever changed my mind and wanted to practice law again, I could pay the regular dues and resume. If I resigned, I wouldn't have to pay anything but—and it was an outcome-determinative but—I would have to take and pass the Bar exam for the second time if I ever wanted to practice again.

When General William Tecumseh Sherman was being touted for the Republican nomination for president in 1884, he rejected the notion with an unambiguous declaration: If nominated, he would not run, and if elected, he would not serve. My attitude toward the Bar exam was much the same. If ordered to take it, I would refuse, and if forced to take it, I would fail. I had forgotten nearly all the law I knew when I passed it more than forty years earlier. I wasn't going to learn it all again, and I wasn't going to take the Bar exam again. My options were to pay fifty dollars and keep my options open or resign and never look back.

Ingalls has been very good to me, but the company has rarely been sued in recent years. Time has marched on, and I doubt they'll ever ask me to do anything again. But if they do, I don't want to have to refuse, which would be especially awkward because Assistant General Counsel Tom Hamrick, the Ingalls official responsible for overseeing my cases, is now my neighbor. He and his wife Aby spend most of their time in New Orleans. When they fled from Hurricane Ida in 2021, they and their three dachshunds stayed in our friend's unoccupied home behind ours in Madison, a Jackson suburb. While they were here, Tom and Aby took a shine to the house and decided to buy it. Their new home will be waiting when the next hurricane comes, and it also serves as a refuge when they get "tired of th[at] dirty old city," to quote Merle Haggard. To avoid the risk that I would have to say no if my friend, client, and neighbor comes calling again, I paid the fifty bucks.

The subtitle of this book says it's stories from my life in the law, but that's not entirely true. All the stories are true, but some don't have much of anything to do with either my life or the law. But it's my book, and I like the stories, so you get what you get. I've been telling many of the stories for decades, and it's fun to write them.

The title of the book is *Trigger Warning*, and here's the first one: Some of the stories in the pages that follow are crude and politically incorrect, especially the ones about sexual harassment cases I defended in the years before workplace Lotharios wised up and became more subtle. I have chosen not to sanitize the stories but instead to tell them exactly as they happened, at least to the best of my recollection.

But I need to add one proviso: I've taken the liberty of changing some names, sometimes to protect the innocent but more often to protect the dishonest, obnoxious, and incompetent. In my long career, I dealt with some lawyers who were all three. I have chosen Dick as the alias for a number of people in the stories. You be the judge. It's a credit to the Mississippi Bar that only one of the Dicks is a Mississippi lawyer.

East Toward Durham

I became a lawyer because I didn't want to be a doctor. That's about all there was to it. Brighter-than-average kids who grew up in small towns in the South in the '60s and '70s were supposed to become doctors or lawyers. I knew I didn't want to be a doctor, so here I am.

I was raised in Tupelo, Mississippi, and went to undergraduate school at the University of Mississippi a/k/a Ole Miss. I majored in political science because it sounded interesting. Not all my classes were easy, but most of them were. I slept late, hung out with my fraternity brothers, skipped a lot of classes, and drank a lot of beer. It wasn't summertime, but the living was easy. It was the four easiest years of my life, at least until I reached the age when I might be retired.

But I studied enough to make good grades and did well on the Law School Admission Test, so I had good options when it came time to choose a law school. I wound up picking Duke over the Universities of Texas and Virginia because Duke gave me a scholarship and a job in the law library for my fiancée, who would be my wife by the time we arrived in Durham. The other schools offered me nothing but a place in the first-year class. Texas wouldn't even send me information about housing. I had to come by and pick it up, the unhelpful woman said. When I told her I was more than 700 miles away and knew no one in Austin who could pick it up and mail it to me, she offered sympathy but no solution. I scratched UT off the list.

I did not apply to law school at Ole Miss. I probably could have gone there on a free ride, but I decided it would be unwise to stay in the same place where I had been sleeping late, hanging out with my fraternity brothers, skipping a lot of classes, and drinking a lot of beer. Because I went to Duke instead, I owed student loans when I graduated and, because I returned to Mississippi to practice, I had to take the Mississippi Bar Exam. Back in the day, and this was way back in the day, graduates of Ole Miss law school had what was called the diploma privilege. They were automatically admitted to the Bar without having to take or pass the Bar exam. It was a sweet perk that was not given to graduates of other law schools.

But I'm very glad I went to Duke. I was surrounded by bright students from all over the country and made lifelong friends. Some of us gather every year to play golf, talk smack, and drink beer, though not as much as my friends and I drank at Ole Miss. We've been taking golf trips for two decades. The first course we played, in Beaufort, South Carolina, is called Secession based on a dubious distinction. South Carolina became the first state to say adios to America with its secession declaration issued on Christmas Eve in 1860. One of my classmates called our trip the Regression at Secession, and the name stuck. I went to our most recent Regression even though I had a bum shoulder and couldn't play. I walked the course with my buddies and made fun of their lousy shots. This time, for the first time, they couldn't make fun of mine.

First Bikini Girl

On May 12, 1979, five days after the last exam of my senior year at Ole Miss, I married Betsy Ann Simpson. You may have noticed I said Carrie was my wife in the prologue. She's #2; Betsy Ann was #1. I tell people I've been married more than forty years, just not consecutive years. The break between marriages lasted just over two years, from December 2008 to New Year's Day 2011.

Betsy Ann and I met on a blind date when I was a freshman at Ole Miss and she was a senior in high school, and we dated the next three years. After our wedding, I worked at a bank in Tupelo for the summer, and she worked at a day camp. We needed to save money to buy furniture, so we lived with my parents.

This is not a marriage guide, but I'll pause here to make a recommendation. Newlyweds should not live with either spouse's parents for the first three months of their marriage. Betsy Ann was always afraid my parents were going to hear us being affectionate. I said we were newlyweds; we were supposed to be affectionate. The situation was suboptimal.

One weekend during the summer, we went to see Betsy Ann's delightful mother, Ann, at her home in Senatobia, ninety miles northwest of Tupelo. I played golf with Betsy Ann's brothers on Saturday. My wedding band was too wide for me to grip a golf club comfortably, so I removed it before we teed off. I didn't have a coin to spot my ball on the greens, so I used the ring. After we finished the round, I searched for the ring in every pocket in my shorts and every compartment in my golf bag. It was nowhere to be found. I went back to the course and retraced my steps on every hole. No luck. Betsy Ann and I decided not to replace the ring right away because our need for a couch and a mattress was more pressing.

At the end of the summer, when Betsy Ann and I moved to North Carolina, Ann made the trip with us. Her plan was to help us get settled, then fly home. We traveled in a caravan. I led the way in a rented U-Haul with Josey, the half English shepherd, half Australian shepherd I had adopted as a puppy the fall before, riding shotgun. Betsy Ann and Ann followed in our used red Datsun 200SX, my first car and a graduation/wedding gift from my parents. We spent the night in Asheville on the way.

The next morning, Betsy Ann and Ann decided to tour the Biltmore estate before continuing east. I was ready to start unpacking and got an early start. When Josey and I arrived in Durham, I circled the campus in search of our destination, Chapel Towers Apartments on Morreene Road. I finally found it, and Josey, who had been cooped up in the cab all morning, was thrilled to be set free. She went racing around our apartment building, and I followed. By the time I caught up, she had a new friend, a very attractive young woman who was lying on a chaise lounge clad in a bikini.

I introduced myself, told her Josey's name, and said we'd just arrived and were moving in. She introduced herself and asked which apartment was ours. After a few minutes of small talk, we parted ways. I moved some things into the apartment, then Josey and I left to see about getting the power turned on.

While we were gone, two things of significance occurred: First, our new friend stuck a note in the door of our apartment inviting Josey and me to join her for dinner that night. Second, Betsy Ann and Ann arrived and found the note. When I returned, an inquisition commenced. I said it was an innocent misunderstanding, which was true, though I left out the part about the bikini. With Betsy Ann standing over me and telling me what to write, I politely declined the invitation and said my wife and I looked forward to getting to know our new neighbor. I stuck it in the door of the apartment where Josey and I would not be having dinner.

The following week, we scraped up enough money to buy me a new wedding band. We bought a narrower one this time so I wouldn't have to remove it to play golf, and I wore it for all twenty-nine years of our marriage. Though we lived in the same apartment building with bikini girl, I never saw her again, at least not in a bikini.

Only Two O'clock Here

My Duke classmates spoke with all sorts of strange accents, which was a brand-new thing for me. I asked one where he went to undergraduate school, and he said UConn. UConn was not yet a basketball powerhouse, and I had no idea UConn was the University of Connecticut. Thinking UConn was Yukon, I had visions of Jack London's "To Build a Fire" and poems by Robert Service. Some of us were talking about religion one day, and another classmate, Alan Gallanty, said he was a kike. I had to ask a friend what that meant. I was not exactly what you would call worldly. My first-ever airline flight was three months before I started law school, when Betsy Ann and I flew to Savannah for our honeymoon on Hilton Head.

I liked my new friends, and law school was much more interesting than undergrad, but at times I wondered if I'd done the right thing by leaving home to attend Duke. I could be going to law school at Ole Miss for free, hanging out with my buddies, drinking a lot of beer, and going home to Tupelo on weekends to see my parents and enjoy home-cooked meals. The internal debate about the wisdom of my choice continued for two or three months. Then one night it ended.

You know what it's like when the phone rings in the middle of the night? When you look at the clock on the bedside table and see that it's three o'clock? And your heart starts racing because you assume something dreadful has happened? Because only bad news comes at three a.m.?

I know what it's like because it happened one weekend in my first semester at Duke. I picked up the phone and, fearing the worst, said hello. Betsy Ann propped herself up on her elbows and waited. Nobody spoke at first, but I could hear music and voices in the background. I said hello again and got a response this time.

"Hey, whatcha doin'?" I recognized the voice. It was one of my fraternity brothers. He'd been drinking a lot of beer.

Worry shifted to anger. "I was sleeping," I answered. "So was Betsy Ann."

The voice on the other end was unapologetic and undeterred. "We were just hanging out and telling stories and thought we'd call and check on you. How you doin'?"

"I was doing fine until the phone rang."

"Come on, man. We just wanted to talk."

"But it's three in the morning."

You know how sometimes somebody says something, and no matter how much time passes, you remember the exact words? This was one of those times. It's been more than forty years, but I remember my drunk buddy's exact words. He said, as if it were an excuse, "But it's only two o'clock here."

I told him to call back at a reasonable hour in the eastern time zone, then hung up. My last thought before I fell back to sleep was that coming to Duke was the right call.

The Outlaw Josey Eason

I grew up with dogs. We adopted Frisky, an Eskimo spitz, when I was six months old. He was my best friend until I was old enough to have two-legged friends. We had more dogs before I left for college and were rarely without one. But Josey was the first one I adopted and the first one who was all mine. I named her for Clint Eastwood's character in *The Outlaw Josey Wales*. Josey died long ago, but when I typed these words Clint was still hanging on.

Josey came to live with me and my roommates in the fall of my senior year at Ole Miss. Baseball fans of a certain age will remember the day, not because of Josey or me, but because it was October 2, 1978, the day an unlikely hero hit a famous home run. The Yankees and Red Sox had finished the '78 season with identical 99–63 records. They played an extra game at Fenway to determine which team would represent the American League East in the playoffs. Yankee shortstop Bucky Dent, who had only five home runs in the 162-game regular season, hit a three-run blast over the Green Monster in the top of the seventh, and the Yankees won 5–4. That same afternoon, Josey moved into the run-down house in Oxford I shared with two fraternity brothers. The Yankees won the World Series two weeks later, and Bucky was named MVP.

Josey was quite popular with my friends and classmates at Duke, and even with people I didn't know. Leash laws weren't a thing yet, and Josey often walked to campus and spent the day lounging on the quad. There were not just students there but other dogs as well. They were called quad dogs and belonged to no one, but they made a handsome living begging for handouts from students. I was told that quad dogs rode the bus between West Campus and East Campus, though I can't say I ever witnessed it. Josey had her name and our phone number on her collar. When I was with her on campus, undergrads who knew her but not me would speak to her by name when we walked by.

When the weather was nice, the law school staff would prop open the front doors. One fine day, when I was in my accustomed spot on the next-to-last row in the large classroom closest to the front door, I heard students in the front of the room laughing. Our professor looked to his right and shook his head. The reason for the laughter soon reached the end of the first row and came into my line of sight. Josey had walked into the front door of the law school, come into our classroom, and was looking for me. She didn't know my schedule, but she knew my scent. I wasn't sure what the professor would think about having a dog in his class, so I decided to sit tight and hope for the best. The professor remained silent as Josey walked up and down the rows trying to find me. But then she ratted me out. When she reached me, she sat down beside me and put her paw on my leg. Our prof shook his head and continued his lecture. Josey stayed until the class ended.

Josey had but one fault. She was young and excitable and would occasionally nip someone who was running or riding a bike. I say nip instead of bite because it wasn't done in anger, and there were no serious injuries. Josey would just get a little too wound up.

My law school softball team was named for Chock full o'Nuts, the coffee chain founded in New York City. Owing to our lack of maturity, we substituted Jock for Chock in the name, but I wasn't responsible. I'd never heard of Chock full o'Nuts and didn't understand the allusion.

Three members of my softball team were victims of Josey's nipping habit. After the third incident, team captain Alan Gallanty observed that the victims all had something in common. We had three Jewish guys on the team, and Josey had nipped them all. Alan and Rob Solomon were two of the victims; I don't remember the third. And not only had Josey nipped all the Jews on the team, but she hadn't laid a tooth on any of the eight Gentiles. Alan accused Josey of being anti-Semitic, but I came to her defense. How could

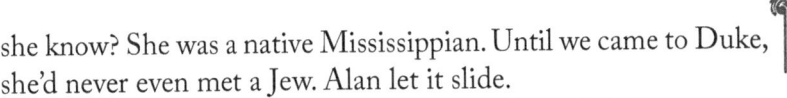

she know? She was a native Mississippian. Until we came to Duke, she'd never even met a Jew. Alan let it slide.

Josey was a fabulous athlete. My friend Doug McCoy, one of the Regression golfers, was our neighbor in Chapel Towers. He and I took turns playing indoor soccer against Josey. She played goalie. She would position herself at one end of the kitchen, and one of us would try to kick a tennis ball past her from the other. She would catch the ball in her mouth or stop it with her chest or a paw, roll it back, then assume the ready position again. Her save-to-goal ratio was impressive.

Josey's most famous display of athleticism resulted in the suspension of an NCAA sports event, a men's soccer game between Duke and arch-rival Carolina. I wasn't there, but another of our Chapel Towers neighbors was delighted to report what he'd witnessed when he came home after the game.

In the middle of the second half, the score tied, Josey somehow managed to get onto the field. She would have come to the sideline if someone had called her, but the overconfident players tried to catch her instead. Nothing could have thrilled her more. The members of the teams may have been Division I athletes, but Josey had twice as many legs and a lower center of gravity. It was a complete mismatch. The game of chase continued until the chasers gave up. Victorious, Josey walked off the field to a rousing ovation.

Don't Want No Raisins

One year during law school, Betsy Ann decided we should go on a health kick. That's usually a New Year's resolution kind of thing, but she chose the beginning of the fall semester for us to change our ways. We ate healthier. I exercised more, lost weight, and looked and felt better.

Because we were trying to live healthy lives, BA decided everybody else in the world should too. She made an announcement in mid-October. Candy is unhealthy, she said, so we weren't going to give it away to trick-or-treaters on Halloween. I asked what we would give them instead. She had considered the matter and had the answer. The treats at our apartment would be miniature boxes of Sun-Maid raisins. I tried to talk her out of it—one night of candy wasn't going to rot a kid's teeth or turn him into an obese diabetic—but she was resolute. Raisins it would be.

Our apartment was a third-floor walk-up. The stairs were on the outside, with landings between floors. When I came home at five o'clock on Halloween, Betsy Ann was already there. It was too early for trick-or-treaters, but we already had a pair. As I was heading up the stairs, two teenage boys were heading down. They were too old for trick-or-treating and weren't wearing costumes, but that didn't stop them. It was Halloween, and who doesn't love a Milky Way?

When I reached the landing between the second and third floors, one of the boys was standing there, peering down into a grocery bag that had been repurposed as a treat-collecting bag. He had a look of anger and disgust on his face. As I walked past, he pronounced his verdict without looking up. "Raisins? Raisins?" he cried out to the Halloween gods, "I don't want no mother-fucking raisins."

I didn't quibble with the young man but instead walked into the apartment and repeated what I'd just heard. I could have said I told you so, but I let the trick-or-treater's words do the talking. We went back to candy the following Halloween and all the ones that came after.

West Toward Home

I spent my career in Mississippi because of a rich couple with bad manners I never met.

I made good grades my first year at Duke and had the opportunity in the fall of my second to interview for summer jobs with excellent firms in Dallas, Atlanta, and New York. The New York firms that interviewed me and my buddy Russ Hardin, another member of the Regression crew, put us up at the Plaza Hotel, and we each lost twenty bucks to a card shark playing three-card monte on the sidewalk.

His loss to the card shark notwithstanding, Russ was much more worldly than I was. He showed me around the city, and I gazed up in wonder at the skyscrapers. We walked into a shop on Park Avenue that sold sexual devices and paraphernalia. I had no idea such places existed. A beautiful young woman in a conservative suit came in, studied the options, and settled on a leather mask festooned with chrome studs. She looked no more self-conscious than if she were buying a loaf of bread. I was a long way from Tupelo. I went on five interview trips that fall, which raised my lifetime number of airline trips to six.

After all my interviews were over, Betsy Ann and I decided Dallas was too flat and treeless and New York too far from home. My favorite firm was King & Spalding in Atlanta. It was and is one of the best firms in the country, and the lawyers who interviewed me were impressive and gracious. I was considering spending half the summer with another firm in another city until Jim Wildman, the K&S partner in charge of recruiting, made me an offer I couldn't refuse. He said Betsy Ann, Josey, and I could house-sit for firm lawyers while they were on vacation, which meant we wouldn't have to rent a place in Atlanta. We would have to keep our apartment in Chapel Towers, and there wouldn't be much left over from my summer salary if we had to pay rent on two apartments. I decided to put all my eggs in one basket and spend the whole summer at K&S.

Shortly before the spring semester ended, Jim called again and said he had good news and bad news. He started with the bad. We wouldn't have a free place for the first month but could sublease an apartment on Peachtree Street being vacated by a firm associate who was getting married. But the good news was very good. For the rest of the summer, we wouldn't be moving from place to place to place but would instead have a palatial home on West Wesley Road in Buckhead all to ourselves. The house, which came with a gardener and housekeeper, was owned by firm clients who were planning to spend the summer in Europe. It wasn't the deal I was promised, but it sounded at least as good. I didn't ask Jim what happened to house-sitting for firm lawyers.

We drove straight to Atlanta after my last exam, and I started work the following Monday. I was making $500 a week at K&S, nearly triple what I'd made in any previous job, and I planned to work every week until classes resumed in August. The work was interesting, I liked the people at the firm, and I enjoyed getting to know my fellow summer clerks. There were seventeen of us from law schools all over the country, and I remain friends with some of them more than four decades later. I was invited to sit in a luxury box at a Braves game, and partners took me to lunch at the Piedmont Driving Club. I became more worldly with each passing day.

Our apartment was the only disappointment. The associate had taken most of his furniture and left only a few things behind. Worse than that, the apartment didn't have central air, and there were no window units. Surely there had been one or more in the past, but they were gone. After suffering through a few hot nights, we were able to borrow a unit that was powerful enough to cool the bedroom to a tolerable temperature if we kept the door closed.

But we were young, it was temporary, and the palace in Buckhead beckoned. It was the bright light at the end of our hot tunnel. We would leave the toasty apartment at night, drive up Peachtree

Street with Josey in the back, turn left on West Wesley, and cruise slowly past our future home. We were casing the joint and counting down the days.

Two days before the countdown was to end, I had conversations with two K&S lawyers named Jim that changed the course of my life. First, Jim Wildman called me into his office with more bad news. The rich couple on West Wesley had not only cancelled their trip to Europe, but they hadn't bothered to tell anyone at the firm. Jim's secretary found out when she called to discuss the details of our stay.

Ah, the rich. Perhaps the couple were like Tom and Daisy Buchanan, careless people who "smashed up things and creatures and then retreated back into their money or their vast carelessness, or whatever it was that kept them together, and let other people clean up the mess they had made." Whatever the cause, other people would have to clean up the mess the couple on West Wesley had made. Jim apologized and said we could rent an apartment for the rest of the summer in a complex where some of the other summer clerks were staying. The couple's inexcusable behavior was not Jim's fault, but the rent was high—seems like a thousand bucks a month—and whatever happened to house-sitting? I told him we were paying rent on our apartment in Durham, and one reason I decided to spend the whole summer at K&S was because we wouldn't have to pay rent on two places. He said he would see what he could do.

The second conversation was with associate Jim Pardo at a reception for the summer clerks that evening. Several years earlier, Jim had spent a year clerking for Charles Clark, who since then had become the Chief Judge of the United States Court of Appeals for the Fifth Circuit. The Fifth Circuit's principal courthouse and administrative staff are in New Orleans, but Judge Clark's home and chambers were in Jackson. Jim had just talked to the judge, who told him he'd hired two clerks for the 1982-83 year but still needed a third. Jim knew I was from Mississippi. He told me Judge Clark was an outstanding judge and a wonderful man and encouraged me to apply.

If the inconsiderate couple on West Wesley hadn't reneged on the deal, I would have thanked Jim Pardo for his advice but disregarded it. I would have cast my lot with King & Spalding and never looked back. But after my talk with Jim Wildman, I was feeling less certain about the firm. I mailed Judge Clark my résumé the next morning.

Jim Wildman soon arranged for us to house-sit for firm lawyers for the rest of the summer. All was well, but when Judge Clark's assistant invited me to come to Jackson for an interview, I couldn't say no. A Jackson firm, Butler Snow, also wanted to meet with me. I scheduled two interviews on the following Friday, with Judge Clark in the morning and Butler Snow after lunch. Betsy Ann and I didn't talk much about spending a year in Jackson or clerking for Judge Clark before my interview with him. We could do that if he offered me the job.

Judge Clark was impressive in both accomplishment and appearance. He had a stellar reputation and had been considered more than once for a seat on the United States Supreme Court. He was also tall and handsome with a thick mane of wavy white hair. He looked like a cross between Charlton Heston and God.

The Chief was all business in the interview. I talked with him first, then with the two secretaries and three current law clerks, then again with him. Near the end, he said he felt very strongly that judges should choose clerks rather than the other way around. He asked if I understood. I didn't really, but I said I did. So, he continued, before he would consider me for the position, he needed my assurance that I would accept the job if he offered it to me. He then stopped and waited for my response.

I wasn't expecting this. Nobody had warned me, and I didn't know what to say. Judge Clark was a fine gentleman. If I had told him I needed to talk to Betsy Ann, I'm sure he would have understood. But I was an unworldly twenty-four-year-old, and he was the God-like Chief Judge of the Fifth Circuit. In the heat of the moment, asking for more time didn't seem like the thing to do. I gave him my answer: "Sure, Judge."

He then said he was meeting with one more candidate right

after lunch and asked how he could reach me that afternoon. I said I was interviewing with Butler Snow, we shook hands, and I was on my way.

Three hours later, while I was meeting with Butler Snow senior litigation partner Larry Frank, his phone rang. His secretary picked it up at her desk and poked her head into the door. Judge Clark was on the phone and wanted to speak with me. Larry excused himself and stepped out. The judge told me he wanted me to clerk with him and that one of his assistants would be in touch with details, including my start date. I thanked him and told him I was looking forward to it. The conversation lasted less than two minutes. I opened Larry's door and invited him back into his own office. I'm sure getting the call from Judge Clark during my interview with a senior partner didn't hurt my prospects with the firm. Butler Snow invited me to work with them the following summer before I started my year with the judge.

Betsy Ann had come with me to Jackson, and we were staying with her cousin. I walked in and broke the news. "Guess what?" I asked. Before she could guess, I told her we were moving to Jackson.

I enjoyed the rest of the summer at King & Spalding and had an easy final year at Duke. Several of us took a class in entrepreneurship in the graduate school of business our last semester. Every Thursday a rich guy came to town, told us how he got rich, answered our questions, then we had happy hour with him. My favorite was Idaho's J. R. Simplot, who among other accomplishments had sold every French fry to McDonald's the massive fast-food chain had ever served.

In the summer after graduation, I worked at two Jackson firms, Butler Snow and the Brunini firm. After the summer ended and I started working for Judge Clark, it came time to decide where I would spend my career. Both Jackson firms were excellent, but I felt more comfortable and had made more friends at Brunini. My decision about a permanent job came down to Brunini versus King & Spalding.

It was a hard call because it was apples and oranges. K&S was a big firm in a big city, 130 lawyers compared to thirty at Brunini.

K&S was more prestigious, and the money would be better, but it was farther from our families, and the cost of living in Atlanta was higher and the traffic worse.

Money wasn't the only factor, but it was definitely a consideration. If memory serves, my starting salary with K&S would be $35,000. At Brunini, it would be $28,000. The difference wasn't enough to be determinative, especially with the difference in the housing market. I wanted to know more, especially the financial difference in the long term, so I asked lawyers at both firms what first-year partners had made the previous year. At K&S it was in the low nineties. At Brunini it was $77,000 plus a car. The firm paid for a Chevy Caprice for each partner. Not exactly my style, but I wasn't going to look a gift car in the grill.

Betsy Ann said the decision was up to me. She would be happy either place. After some sleepless nights, I decided the money difference wasn't enough to overcome our wanting to live in Mississippi and be close to our families. I decided on Brunini, walked into my office in Judge Clark's chambers the next morning, and immediately made three calls: two painful ones to King & Spalding and Butler Snow, then a happy one to Brunini.

With a crystal ball, I might have chosen differently. Seven years later, when I was a first-year partner at Brunini, I made $79,000, but the firm's accountants had put the kibosh on firm cars. A Caprice Classic was no longer part of the deal. In the meantime, I was keeping up with friends at King & Spalding who were now first-year partners there, and I asked what they made. Over the intervening seven years, while first-year partner compensation at Brunini went up by two grand but down by a car, the compensation for beginning partners at K&S nearly tripled. The year I made $79,000, my King & Spalding classmates earned $250,000. I kicked myself for asking and chalked it up to *c'est la vie.* More than thirty years later, I asked again. The difference had grown to seven figures. I kicked and chalked again.

Here's one more King & Spalding story before I turn to my post-law-school life in Mississippi.

I became friends with a young King & Spalding associate named Charlie Ogburn during my summer in Atlanta. Seems like he was the one who loaned us the window unit to make the apartment more bearable. I thank him for that and for telling me this story.

President Jimmy Carter, who like Clint Eastwood is still among the living as I type these words, had many close relationships with King & Spalding lawyers. Several left the firm to serve in key positions in his administration. Griffin Bell was his Attorney General, Jack Watson his Chief of Staff. Another K&S partner, Charles Kirbo, was his personal attorney. During the Carter administration, the firm held a reception for the President and First Lady, where they met many of the firm's attorneys, including Charlie Ogburn.

A year or so after that event, Jimmy and Rosalynn came to K&S's Atlanta offices to meet with Charles Kirbo about family business. The meeting was in a conference room on the twenty-sixth floor. No reception was planned, and the visit was unannounced. When it came time for lunch, Kirbo said he needed to run down the stairs to his office on the twenty-fifth to get his jacket. He would meet the Carters in the elevator lobby. Along the way, Kirbo got detained.

Charlie Ogburn's office was also on the twenty-fifth floor. He was hard at work with a deadline looming when noon came, and he decided to leave the office, grab a sandwich, and bring it back to his office and eat at his desk. He walked out to the elevator lobby and hit the down button.

When the door opened, what to his wondering eyes should appear, but the President of the United States, the First Lady, and two Secret Service agents. But what Charlie heard was even more startling than what he saw. The president, thinking Kirbo would be walking into the lobby at any second, called out, "Come on, Charlie, let's get some lunch."

Charlie Ogburn, marveling at the president's uncanny memory for names, responded, "No thank you, Mr. President, I don't have time."

Bob Morrison was a young corporate attorney at Brunini, two or three classes ahead of me. He was one of my favorite lawyers at the firm and one of the main reasons I decided to spend my career there. Bob loved telling jokes. Indeed, he loved telling them so much that he told the same ones over and over. His delivery was funnier than the jokes were. He invariably laughed louder than those of us on the receiving end.

After I accepted Brunini's offer but was still clerking for Judge Clark, I had two memorable lunches with Bob. I remember the first one because of four shoes that didn't fit and four shoes that did.

I had a pair of black Allen Edmonds wingtips that were six or seven years old but looked brand new. My daddy had bought them for me at Progressive Shoe Store in Pontotoc, twenty miles west of Tupelo. I chose a pair that was too tight because I assumed they would stretch like my cheaper shoes did. But I was wrong. The wingtips didn't stretch, and they hurt my feet, so I hardly ever wore them. Thus the brand-new appearance.

But the shoes were too expensive to give away, so I carried them with me through life, from Mississippi to North Carolina and Georgia, then back to Mississippi. Once a year or so, hoping for a miracle, I would give them another try. But there was no miracle. My feet didn't shrink, the shoes didn't grow, and they still hurt my feet.

My annual day of miracle-hoping came around again in the fall of 1982. Bob and Walter Weems, another Brunini lawyer, invited me to join them for lunch at the Elite, an old Jackson establishment on Capitol Street. They were already there when I arrived, so they didn't see me limping, but after we finished and paid the tab, there was no hiding my stupidity. As we headed up the sidewalk, I was walking gingerly and wincing in pain. When Walter asked what was wrong, I confessed that my shoes were too little and always had been. He politely refrained from asking why I bought them and why I was wearing them.

We continued at a slow pace, and I noticed Bob was looking down at my shoes. I thought it was odd, but after another half block, he said something that explained his interest. His shoes, it so happened, were a little too big.

What were the odds? We then took the obvious next step. We sat down on the steps of the nearest building, the 111 Capitol Building, and swapped shoes. Voilà! Just like that, we both went from shoes that didn't fit to shoes that did. I walked the rest of the way to the federal courthouse with a bounce in my step.

Bob's former shoes immediately became my go-to shoes for court, church, weddings, and funerals. I had them resoled three times before they finally wore out after fifteen years of constant use. When they did, I boxed them up, mailed them to Bob, and thanked him for letting me borrow them.

While writing this, I came across a copy of the letter I sent Bob when I returned his shoes. Because Bob loved jokes, I closed the letter with one: Two brothers, ages nine and six, decided it was high time they started cussing. They made a vow. The next morning, when they came down for breakfast, the older one would say hell, the younger one ass. When they walked into the kitchen, they could see their mother was in a foul mood, but a promise is a promise. When she asked the older one what he wanted, he gulped hard and declared, "Hell, I'll just have a bowl of Cheerios." Mom's eyes narrowed, her face reddened, and she backhanded him, knocking him to the floor. She then turned to his little brother and asked, "What about you, young man?" He gulped even harder. "I don't know," he said, "but you can bet your sweet ass it won't be Cheerios."

The second memorable lunch explains why I had to mail the shoes to Bob and couldn't just hand them to him. This time it was just the two of us, and what he had to say was more painful than my shoes. I was looking forward to finishing my clerkship with Judge Clark, spending my career with Bob at Brunini, and laughing as he told the same jokes over and over. But it was not to be. He was leaving the firm to work in his family business in Vicksburg and was gone from Brunini before I arrived. It was c'est la vie all over again.

My Year With The Chief

I had a great year with Judge Clark. He was a brilliant man and an outstanding judge. His mission in every case was to study the law and the facts and do his best to decide it correctly. If he ever got one wrong, I don't know about it.

I'm certain my one year with the Chief was more beneficial to my career than my three years of law school. I didn't learn as much law from him as I did at Duke, but I learned far more about how to practice law and conduct myself as a lawyer. My experience assisting the decision maker was invaluable. I learned always to play it straight—that stretching the law or the facts is not just wrong, but it will ruin your credibility and destroy your client's case.

Judge Clark had sympathy for lawyers who lacked ability but none for those who were unethical or dishonest. A lawyer cited a prior decision by the Fifth Circuit in a brief and claimed it established a legal principle that seemed doubtful. The published opinions from the Fifth Circuit and other courts were still in books then, and the judge asked me to retrieve the volume containing the decision. As we suspected, the lawyer had misrepresented the holding. Judge Clark asked for a copy so he would have it with him on the bench when the case was argued in New Orleans the following week. When he pulled out the decision and confronted the lawyer, I was sitting in the courtroom. It was painful for the lawyer but a valuable lesson for me. I never wanted to be on the receiving end of anything like that.

Some of the judges on the Fifth Circuit—John Brown and Irving Goldberg in particular—tried to write entertaining opinions. Judge Clark could have gone quip to quip with them, but he believed every case was too important to the parties for judges to do anything suggesting they didn't take it seriously. But in one case, he let me push the envelope.

It was a criminal case, an appeal from a conviction for bank robbery in north Mississippi. The robber had fled with the cash in his car, but a teller had included a packet of bait money that was timed to explode. The robber thought he'd made a clean getaway, but then the bait money blew up. He and his clothes and the inside of his car were spattered with red dye.

Flush with cash, the robber changed clothes and went out drinking to celebrate. He was still in the bar when the cops found him. His clothes were clean, but his hands were not. When I described the case to Pamela Morris, the wonderful woman who was my secretary when I worked for the judge, she responded with a comment that served as an inspiration for the first line of the opinion I drafted for the court. I wrote: "Caught red-handed is usually only a cliché. No so here."

After giving the Chief my draft, I waited for him to return it with his edits. I wondered if my opening words would survive his pen. When he handed it back, he was smiling. I looked down; the robber was still caught red-handed.

I also drafted the opinion in *Richards v Allstate*, in which the court affirmed a jury verdict of $375,000 in punitive damages based on Allstate's refusal to pay $2,500 in proceeds on a car insurance policy. The relevant principle of Mississippi law, which was established only a few years earlier, was that refusal to pay proceeds under an insurance policy without a legitimate or arguable basis constitutes an independent tort for which punitive damages may be awarded.

My last day with Judge Clark was July 15, 1983. Less than two weeks later, I took the Mississippi Bar Exam over a span of three days. It's rare to be excited by a test question, but I was thrilled when I read the first question on the torts section of the exam. The question was based on the Fifth Circuit's decision in *Richards v. Allstate*. I cited all the relevant precedents in my answer and described the opinion I'd drafted as well-written and well-reasoned.

At the lunch break, friends who were taking the exam with me said they were baffled by the question, particularly why it was on the torts section. They were unaware of the new independent-tort doctrine and viewed the insurance company's failure to pay the proceeds under the policy as a garden-variety breach of contract. When I explained the principle and how I knew about it, I was, at least briefly, no longer their friend.

Judge Clark remained on the court for nearly a decade after I finished my year with him. Before he retired, lawyers often asked me if they should want Judge Clark on the panel assigned to a case. I had a standard response: He's going to get it right, so if it's a case you should win, you want him, but if it's a case you should lose, you don't. The Chief was what a judge should be.

Two-Legged Mr. Ed

Ed Brunini, Sr. was what a lawyer should be. He was a gifted advocate, a trusted advisor, and a respected leader. Senators Jim Eastland and John Stennis came to him for advice, as did a series of Mississippi's governors. He was chosen to lead the state's relief efforts after Hurricane Camille and was instrumental in establishing two important Jackson institutions, St. Dominic Hospital and Mississippi College School of Law. He undoubtedly did more than any other lawyer to make the Brunini firm a success, but he chose to be paid less than his contributions warranted. He loved the firm and his partners and cared little about material wealth.

The younger lawyers in the firm called him Mr. Ed. That's what I called him in the 1980s, so that's what I'll call him now. Whether he or the talking horse on television was Mr. Ed first, I can't say. They were both Mr. Ed by the time I saw one on TV and met the other one.

Roman Catholics of Italian descent were as rare as hen's teeth in central Mississippi, but if that was an obstacle to Mr. Ed's success, he overcame it with wisdom and charm. He was a kind man, loved a good story, and could hold forth at length on a wide variety of subjects. And though he was devoutly religious—his brother Joseph was the bishop—he was no teetotaler. He enjoyed the "oil of conversation," the name bestowed on libations by Mississippi legislator Soggy Sweat in his magnificent Whiskey Speech. If you don't know the speech, look it up. You'll thank me.

I learned Mr. Ed enjoyed a toddy when he took me to lunch while I was clerking for the firm in the summer of 1982. When we walked into the lobby of the Petroleum Club, he surprised me by turning right toward the bar instead of left toward the dining room. We sat down and, without waiting for either of us to speak, a waiter brought him a martini on the rocks. This wasn't Mr. Ed's first visit to the bar at the Petroleum Club. Ten minutes later, he held up his empty glass, and the waiter replaced it with a full one. But that was the limit. When he finished the second one, we walked back through the lobby to the dining room.

Mr. Ed was already in his seventies when I met him and was nearly as retired as I am now. But he had one last case, and it was a big one. Though nationwide prohibition was repealed in 1933, Mississippi and other states in the Bible Belt chose to remain dry. The sale and possession of alcohol were banned here until the mid-1960s. A coalition of strange bedfellows, Baptists and bootleggers, supported the ban. Like nationwide prohibition, the Mississippi law was honored in the breach. Bootleggers thrived.

The law was finally changed in 1966. The new statute did not repeal statewide prohibition but instead created a local option. Counties were permitted to opt out of the ban and legalize the sale of alcohol under strict regulations established by the state.

Fifteen years later, just over half of Mississippi's counties had chosen to exercise the option. Liquor stores sprung up just over the county line in wet counties adjacent to dry ones. If someone in a dry county said he was going "to the line," the purpose of the mission was understood. Laws often have unintended consequences. The local-option law led many in dry counties to head to the nearest wet one, buy their booze of choice, and drink it on the drive home.

One of the regulations imposed by the state was a sweeping prohibition on advertising. Even in counties where alcoholic beverages could be sold, they could not be advertised. A group of businesses filed suit in 1980 challenging the prohibition on first-amendment grounds. Those who brought the case were not owners of wineries, distilleries, or liquor stores, who preferred to keep the money they would otherwise spend on ads fighting for market share. The plaintiffs, all in the business of advertising, were the potential recipients of that money. The lead plaintiff was Lamar Outdoor Advertising, which was in the billboard business.

Mr. Ed was never a member of the legislature, but he sometimes played a role in crafting legislation and negotiating the compromises necessary to ensure its passage. So it was with the 1966 local-option law. And when the advertising ban was challenged on constitutional grounds, Mr. Ed volunteered to represent the state and lead the effort to uphold the ban. I suspect he and the firm handled the litigation for free.

The plaintiffs won in the lower court, and a panel of the Fifth Circuit affirmed the ruling. The opinion was published in March 1983, during my year with Judge Clark. Mr. Ed and the lawyers working with him then filed a petition for *en banc* review, a procedure that allows all the judges on the court, not just a three-judge panel, to consider a case. The petition was granted, and I was in New Orleans for the oral argument in the court's magnificent *en banc* courtroom.

Later that summer, before the full court ruled, Mr. Ed tracked me down at a firm function to pick my brain about the oral argument. He had seen me in the courtroom. He said he realized I didn't know how the case would turn out, but he was interested to know which arguments I thought were most persuasive.

But he was wrong; I did know how the case would turn out. The judges voted immediately after the argument, and responsibility for writing the majority and dissenting opinions was assigned. I told Mr. Ed I knew the outcome but didn't say what it was. His eyes got big, and he cleared his throat. He wanted to know in the worst sort of way, but he knew it would be improper to ask, so he didn't. And if he had, I would have said I couldn't tell him. I wouldn't have been caught off guard as I had been two summers earlier when Judge Clark asked if I would take the job if he offered it. Two months later, on Halloween, Mr. Ed won his last case by a vote of eight to five. The opinion can be found in the Federal Reporter at 718 F. 2d 738.

Mr. Ed continued coming to the office after his last case, offering advice, telling stories, going through old files to write a history of the firm, and having two martinis at lunch. One day he came across an announcement from a firm in Yazoo City that is now Henry, Barbour, DeCell and Bridgforth. The announcement

was from the 1940s and congratulated a new lawyer on joining the firm.

Federal district judge William Barbour, who was appointed to the bench during my year with Judge Clark, was a member of the Henry Barbour firm before then. Mr. Ed was a thoughtful man and knew Judge Barbour would appreciate receiving the announcement. He could have sent the announcement himself, but he was also a generous man, and he knew I would benefit from having a good relationship with the judge. He brought the announcement to me, and I sent it to Judge Barbour with a note about Mr. Ed's work on the history of our firm. I received a gracious note in return.

Bill Goodman was the Ed Brunini of Watkins & Eager, or maybe it was the other way around. Like Mr. Ed, Bill was a brilliant lawyer and leader of his firm. His contributions to his firm, church, and profession, like those of Mr. Ed, were invaluable. When Bill died in 2021, his obituary stated that he would be well remembered for his warmth, intellect, wit, knack for storytelling, and deep love for his family. The same could be said of Mr. Ed.

I had the pleasure of working with Bill only once. Early in my career, he was brought into a big commercial case and helped the parties negotiate a settlement. Not long after the ink was dry, I had lunch one day at the Petroleum Club with Leigh Allen, a senior partner at Brunini. Bill was also there, sitting at another table. When Leigh and I stood up to leave, Bill motioned for us to come over to his table. He greeted both of us, but his purpose was to speak to Leigh about me. He said he hoped Leigh and his partners realized what a fine young lawyer I was and how much money I was making for them.

More than thirty-five years have passed since Mr. Ed brought me the announcement and Bill spoke to Leigh about me, but I have not forgotten. Both were kind gestures to a young lawyer just learning to make his way. Many other young lawyers no doubt benefitted from their kindness. Ed Brunini and Bill Goodman were outstanding lawyers, but they were better men.

Rocky Start

Who needs a lawyer? Not Jerry Lynn Young, that's for sure.

President Reagan nominated Jackson labor lawyer Grady Jolly to the Fifth Circuit in 1982. He was confirmed by the Senate two weeks after I began my clerkship with Judge Clark. Judge Jolly served as an active judge on the court for exactly thirty-five years, from his forty-fifth birthday to his eightieth. When I wrote these lines, he was eighty-five but still a senior judge.

Judge Jolly is a delightful man, a raconteur and lover of good books and stories. He enjoys hearing them and excels at telling them. I came to know him because his chambers in Jackson were not yet ready when he was sworn in. He and his law clerks used Judge Clark's library during the year of my clerkship. I owe Judge Jolly a debt of gratitude for introducing me to Soggy Sweat's Whiskey Speech. If you looked it up as I recommended in the last chapter, you owe debts of gratitude to the late legislator, the judge, and me.

In my first year at Brunini, Judge Jolly appointed me to handle an appeal pending in the Fifth Circuit. He didn't ask if I was interested; he just did it. My client was Jerry Lynn Young, a convicted felon serving time in Parchman Penitentiary in the Mississippi Delta. Like the defendant who was caught red-handed, Jerry Lynn was convicted of robbing a bank. The bank was in Tupelo, which may be why Judge Jolly thought of me. I never asked.

Unlike the red-handed robber, Jerry Lynn was prosecuted in state court, not federal, where he was represented by a public defender. The jury convicted him, and he was sentenced to thirty years in prison. His lawyer appealed, but the conviction was affirmed by the Mississippi Supreme Court.

The Supreme Court's decision left Jerry Lynn up a creek without a paddle. He was behind bars, no longer had a lawyer, and had reached the end of the line in state court. But he did not give up. He had time on his hands and became a jailhouse lawyer. He researched the law, marshaled his arguments, and filed a pro se (meaning without a lawyer) petition for a writ of habeas corpus (an order releasing him) in federal court in north Mississippi.

Surprisingly, the district judge granted Jerry Lynn's petition, finding that he was denied his right to due process because of testimony from an eyewitness that was based on an impermissibly suggestive pretrial photo identification. The court ordered the state to release him or promptly retry him. The state appealed, and Judge Jolly appointed me to represent Jerry Lynn in the Fifth Circuit.

I never met Jerry Lynn, but I spoke with him several times as I drafted the brief on his behalf. He was bright and grateful for my efforts, and the brief I wrote was good, or at least I thought so at the time. But victory was not to be. Without hearing oral argument, the Fifth Circuit reversed the district court's decision and denied Jerry Lynn's quest for freedom.

The court did not find that the photo identification was proper. The judges instead concluded that relief should have been denied in the district court because the Mississippi Supreme Court had found that Jerry Lynn's trial lawyer did not make a proper objection to the photo identification. Testimony from three accomplices that Jerry Lynn robbed the bank didn't help. Nor did that from a gun salesman who identified Jerry Lynn as the purchaser of the shotguns found with the stolen money.

I lost other cases in the decades that followed, but I never lost another one that meant my client would remain in a prison cell. When I notified Jerry Lynn, he was disappointed though, to his credit, he did not blame me. But when I broke the news to him, I wondered what he must have thought about not only me but my entire profession. His record when he was represented by members of the Bar trained in the law was 0–3, the final loss caused by a mistake by the lawyer in the first one. By contrast, Jerry Lynn was undefeated, 1–0, when there was no lawyer around to screw things up.

After talking to Jerry Lynn, I pondered my future. What did it say about me that I couldn't even win a case my client had won without a lawyer? Nothing good, that's for sure. It was an inauspicious beginning to my career as a litigator. My appointment to represent Jerry Lynn was over, and I never spoke to him again.

Life Lessons

Life Lesson Number 1: You have to make every important decision in life before you know enough to make it. Whether and where to go to college, what to study, what to do for a living, where to live, and many others. You can't possibly know everything you need to know to decide those things, and I sure didn't. I've counseled my children and grandchildren to do better than I did, to learn everything they can, to spend time with people who do what they think they may want to do for a living.

Because I didn't know enough, I chose not to begin my career at Brunini as a litigator. With the benefit of forty years of hindsight, it's obvious my decision was foolish. I'm very competitive, but my attention span is variable at best and minuscule at worst. If you think I'm being too hard on myself, you should ask the younger lawyers who worked with me. They would tell you about all the times I told them to start over when they were explaining something because my mind had drifted out to sea. I needed competition and the risk of losing to stay focused. I also enjoyed the creativity involved in litigating cases, in deciding what arguments to make and how to make them.

But I knew none of that when I started at Brunini in August 1983. Even after three years of law school and a fourth clerking for Judge Clark, I still didn't know what kind of law I wanted to practice. I chose to join the firm's commercial department, to work on transactions instead of lawsuits. It was a mistake. I found most of the work boring and tedious and, because I found it boring and tedious, I wasn't especially good at it. I questioned why I'd gone to law school. A friend suggested I interview with another firm. I said it wasn't the firm, it was the work.

But there were breaks from the boredom. My most interesting project was helping to restructure a long-distance telephone business. I was a rookie, and the partner in charge, Leigh Allen, let me do things he probably shouldn't have. I attended meetings in Tampa, New Orleans, and Louisville and negotiated the terms of several transactions.

Our principal client on the project was a Jackson businessman named Steve. One of the older partners at Brunini was younger than Mr. Ed but not by much. He still came to the office nearly every day but no longer did any work to speak of. His office was next to mine. Steve told me at some point that the older partner was his distant cousin.

When Steve and I flew home after one of our meetings, he flew first class, so I did too. After I had a couple of Scotches and my guard was down and my tongue was loose, Steve asked me about his cousin. Specifically, he wanted to know if he still did any work. My answer went something like this: "Not a lick. He comes in at ten or eleven, reads the paper, then meets some buddies for a liquid lunch, gets hammered, stumbles back to the office, closes his door, sleeps it off, then goes home." It was the gospel truth, but I soon wished I hadn't told it.

I was reading a document in my office a week or two later when I heard a man clear his throat. I looked up. Steve's cousin was standing in my doorway, smiling. He said, "My cousin Steve told me what you said about me." I felt my face get hot. I had to say something, so I went with something like this: "You know that Steve; you can't ever tell about him." I don't remember what the cousin said next, but the conversation soon ended. He didn't tell me what Steve had told him, and I sure didn't ask.

Days of trepidation followed as I waited for the axe to fall. I imagined the scene: The firm's managing partner would summon me to his office and instruct me to close the door. He would tell me to sit, then say, "It has come to our attention that you told a client that one of our senior partners is a drunk. Is that true?" I would confess, and he would fire me on the spot.

But days went by, then weeks. I passed Steve's cousin in the hall, and he greeted me as if nothing had happened. I decided I was in the clear and breathed a sigh of relief. I survived unscathed, and I learned Life Lesson Number 2: Be careful what you say and to whom you say it. One New Year's I resolved to say fewer of the things that occurred to me to say. I should have made the resolution before Steve asked me about his cousin.

Turning Crushed Steel into Hoops of Steel

Betty May Collins, Betsy Ann's great-aunt, was an extraordinary woman. She graduated from college when she was only eighteen, became a professor, and taught students who were older than she was. She was on the faculty at what is now the University of Memphis for many years. She became a renowned thespian in local theater and starred in many plays. She trained newscasters in elocution and appeared in commercials, most notably as the little old lady who blew up cars with dynamite for Bluff City Buick. She married for the first and only time when she was seventy-eight. When Betsy Ann and I visited her in Memphis, she sectioned our grapefruit to save us the trouble. She never, I'm certain, gave raisins to trick-or-treaters on Halloween.

We traded in my Datsun for a Mazda GLC when we moved to Jackson. We were making payments on it with interest at nearly seventeen percent, but we needed a second car after I started at Brunini in 1983. We couldn't afford much, but we could afford Aunt Betty's 1968 Volkswagen Beetle. We bought it for $800, which was fair market value. It was old, and the seat belts didn't work, but it ran. I drove it from home to the office and back until July 10, 1986, when I made it to the office but didn't make it back.

I know the exact date because the car met its end that day and I nearly met mine. I was driving home from work on West Street in the left lane alongside Millsaps College. When I topped a hill, I saw two cars stopped in front of me, the first one waiting to turn left, the second one behind it. I checked the right lane, saw it was clear, and changed lanes without slowing down. Right when I did, the driver of the second car decided to change lanes too. But he was starting from a dead stop, and I was going forty. To keep from rear-ending him, I swerved to the left. It was yet another mistake, and this one was nearly fatal. I hit a car coming the other way head on.

If you must have a head-on collision and can choose the vehicle to be driving, I don't recommend an old VW Bug with broken seat belts. Based on my subsequent diagnoses, my head obviously hit the windshield and my knee the dashboard. A police car and ambulance arrived promptly, but neither the cops nor the EMTs could open the VW's doors. The car was crushed, and I was stuck inside. Another crew, this one equipped with jaws of life, was summoned. During the delay, a crowd gathered, and the press appeared. A photo of me in my smushed Bug appeared in the Jackson *Clarion-Ledger* the next day.

Because I was addle-brained from whacking my head, I have no first-hand knowledge of what happened next. But I was not unconscious, as subsequent events make clear. The jaws of life freed me, and I was loaded into the ambulance and whisked away to the University of Mississippi Medical Center. It was there that I became the master of my fate.

I don't remember my motives because I don't remember anything, but with hindsight I came up with two possibilities. Friends had gone to med school at UMMC and told me stories about the place that did not inspire confidence. Did those stories come to mind when the ambulance pulled up at the ER? There's no way to know. My second possible motive was more mercenary. For many years, the Brunini firm had represented St. Dominic Hospital, which was just down the road from UMMC. I had learned in my three years with the firm that it's good business to do business with clients. We were often reminded by firm elders that we should bind our clients to the firm with "hoops of steel." Did that occur to me as I lay in the ambulance surrounded by EMTs? Again, there's no way to know.

But for some reason, I refused to let the EMTs remove me from the ambulance and take me inside. I told the driver there'd been a change in plans and instructed him to make a U-turn and take me to St. Dominic. I must have been insistent because the driver complied. Again, this is all according to what I was told, though I can attest that I was in a room at St. Dominic when my brain came unaddled.

The CEO of St. Dominic at the time was a man named Frank Quiriconi. I had spoken to him a time or two and done some legal work for the hospital. When I was wheeled into the ER, I was promptly given a neurological assessment to determine just how addled my brain was. What was my name? My wife's name? My date of birth? I evidently scored quite well until I was asked to name the president. They were looking for the President of the United States, but I said Frank Quiriconi. For someone who had just been knocked senseless, I must say that was pretty smart.

Before too long, Betsy Ann arrived, then colleagues from work. And then came the star of the show. Word had reached Pamela Morris, my lovely secretary from my year with Judge Clark, that the clerk she called Baby Brooks had been in a bad car wreck. Before receiving the call, she had come home from work and slipped into something more comfortable. Without taking the time to change back into something more modest, she raced to the hospital.

It is often said that no good deed goes unpunished. Well, not in this case. My Brunini colleagues who had come to the hospital to see about me were well rewarded for their good deed when Pamela arrived on the scene. She was, so I was told, wearing short shorts and a halter top, and I was no longer the center of attention. When I returned to work a week later, my buddies were still thinking and talking about her. They would ask an obligatory question or two about my recovery, then turn to the subject that really interested them. One, alluding with alliteration to Pamela, asked, "Who was that wasp-waisted woman?"

I was transferred from the ER to a regular room and soon regained my senses. In the meantime, word of my wreck and subsequent conduct reached Frank Quiriconi. He learned not only that I had refused treatment at UMMC and demanded to be taken to his hospital, but that I had declared that he, not Ronald Reagan, was the president. He called to check on me, then came to see me. Word spread. Talk about your hoops of steel. The entire episode was an object lesson in good client relations, though I don't recommend it.

My two primary injuries were a brain hemorrhage and a cracked kneecap, which sound worse than they were. I soon recovered, my head faster than my knee. But there were several times when the hemorrhage, or at least the diagnosis of it, came in handy.

I've always been good with dates and numbers but terrible with names. As for numbers, I still remember the birthdays and phone numbers of my childhood friends. When Carrie told me her new phone number ended in 1706, I said that was the year Benjamin Franklin was born. When my daughter said my granddaughter would be the circus barker at her preschool program on February 12, 2009, I told her that was Abraham Lincoln's 200th birthday. Carrie says I'm a nerd. I prefer savant.

But I'm no savant with names. I can't tell you a person's name five minutes after hearing it, and I forget the names of people I've known for forty years. I was terrible with names both before and after the wreck, but when it happened after, I had an excuse. I would say, "I'm sorry. You may have heard about my wreck. What's your name again?"

Flexible Entendre

Here's a story about another attractive woman, one who clerked for Judge Clark and worked with Pamela two or three years after I did. My first cousin Leslie Bobo was quite attractive. Because she was my cousin, I wasn't supposed to notice, but I did. I tell you she was attractive because it's important to the story.

Leslie went to law school at Emory, did very well, and Judge Clark hired her to clerk for him after she graduated. When Leslie began her year with the Chief, our firm's recruiting committee asked me to find out her plans for the future. If she was interested in a career with Brunini, I was to schedule an interview. I invited her to lunch at the Petroleum Club to fulfill my assignment.

This was the mid-1980s, and times were different then. The Petroleum Club occupied the top two floors of Capital Towers in downtown Jackson. The nineteenth floor was divided between the main dining room and the bar where Steve's cousin drank his lunch and Mr. Ed took me. The twentieth floor was less formal, served sandwiches, and had two pool tables on which I shot many a game. The club was segregated, not by race but by sex. Women were allowed on the nineteenth floor but not the twentieth. In keeping with the club's name, men in the oil and gas business gathered there.

Leslie and I had lunch in the main dining room and discussed her future. She was interested in the firm and said she could walk across the street from the courthouse to our offices in the Trustmark Building for an interview most any time. Leslie's father, Tom Joyner, worked at a commercial insurance agency on the sixteenth floor of Capital Towers. After we finished lunch and were walking to the elevator lobby, Leslie said she was going to stop and see him before going back to work. I pushed the down button, and we waited.

The doors opened, and neither President Carter nor the First Lady was in the elevator. Instead, four or five older men were heading down from the twentieth floor. They looked to be oil guys. We exchanged perfunctory greetings and nods, and they sized up Leslie. She pushed the button for sixteen, and we rode down the three floors in silence. When the doors opened again, Leslie stepped out, turned, and thanked me for lunch. Then, with a winsome smile, she added, "And remember, I'm flexible." With that, the doors closed.

We continued our silent descent. One of the men in the elevator was obviously quite taken with the combination of Leslie's beauty and her parting comment. As we neared the ground floor, he said, "Um-hum, I bet she is."

The Devil Made Me Do It

Leslie Bobo and Johnny Wade were born on the same day in January 1958 and grew up together in Jackson. Johnny and Joel Bobo, Leslie's future husband, were a class behind me in the fraternity at Ole Miss. A year after I left for Duke, Johnny started law school at Ole Miss. He and I reunited when we had summer jobs at the Brunini firm in 1982. I had graduated and was about to start my clerkship with Judge Clark. Johnny had finished his second year of law school and still had one to go. A year later, after he graduated and I completed my year with the Chief, we reunited again as associates at the firm.

Because I went to Duke and Johnny went to Ole Miss, I owed student loans and had to take the Bar exam, and he didn't and didn't. Johnny joined the firm's litigation department immediately, but it took me several years to see the light and decide I wanted to be a litigator. Some would look at his life choices and mine and say he's smarter than I am.

Johnny and I practiced together at Brunini for twenty-two years. He's still there as of this writing, but in 2005 I left for pastures that were sometimes greener but sometimes weren't. The firm I joined that year, McGlinchey Stafford, was based in New Orleans. Three months after I made the move, I watched in alarm as CNN reported that Hurricane Katrina was flooding my new firm's home city. Johnny seemed way smarter than I was then.

There were not only sex-segregated downtown clubs in Jackson in the 1980s, but there were also law firms, including Brunini, that paid their associates based entirely on seniority. Every associate in the same class received the same salary. The reward for long hours and high-quality work was not more money in the short term but

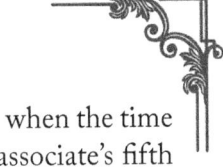

the prospect of an invitation to join the partnership when the time came. At Brunini, that was on March 1 after the associate's fifth anniversary at the firm.

The March 1 date was because the firm was on a fiscal year that began then. Associates would receive annual raises effective on March 1, but they wouldn't be reflected on their paychecks until March 15. Firm management had a great deal to tend to at the end of the fiscal year and usually didn't consider the matter of associate raises until early March. Speculation, curiosity, and tension mounted as payday on the 15th approached.

Early 1988 was an especially tense time for Johnny and me as well as Rod Clement, who joined the firm when we did. We started in the summer of 1983, and our last year as associates was beginning. Generous raises would be a good sign we were on track to become partners the following year. Johnny had an additional reason to be anxious. His wife Jan was pregnant with the second of their three daughters and had quit her job. For the foreseeable future, the Wades would be a single-income family. Johnny had a keen interest in knowing just how much that income would be.

Less than a week before the 15th, I had lunch with a group of associates at the Mayflower, a Greek restaurant that has been a fixture in downtown Jackson for nearly a century. The group included Rod but not Johnny, who was in Houston on business. Rod had done some snooping about our raises and had news to report. Firm management would not be able to decide by the 15th. The checks we would receive in a few days would be at our old salaries. We would get caught up with our paychecks at the end of the month.

You remember that scene in *Animal House*? The one where the guy's in bed with the girl at the toga party and she passes out? And the devil appears, then an angel? And the devil urges him to take full advantage of the situation, but the angel counsels him against it? Well, when Rod told us our raises would be delayed, it was the devil who appeared to me. No angel came.

Johnny and I both enjoyed practical jokes. He once placed an ad in the paper for a garage sale at the home of an unsuspecting friend. To lure the maximum number of early shoppers, the ad said, "Multi-family garage sale. Come early, stay late, free donuts while they last." Johnny was so pleased with himself that he rose before dawn on the day of the faux sale, erected signs pointing the way to the friend's house, then hid in the bushes and waited. He was well rewarded when shoppers came rolling in just before dawn, found no donuts and nothing for sale, and rang his buddy's doorbell. His buddy spotted one of the signs in his yard, marched out, ripped it up, and threw it down in disgust. Johnny waited till he was back inside and put it back up.

Johnny and I had played a number of practical jokes on each other. It was now my turn, and the news from Rod presented a golden opportunity. I swore everyone at the Mayflower to secrecy about the delay in our raises and began hatching a plan. By the time the 15th rolled around, half the firm was in on it.

My principal co-conspirator was Perry Sansing, an associate a year behind Johnny and me and one of our good buddies. If Johnny called Perry from Houston and asked about our raises, Perry would say I'd heard some news about a change the firm was making but hadn't told him the details. Sure enough, Johnny called, and Perry played his role to perfection. And Johnny, who was hungry for information, took the bait. I left the office early that afternoon and went home to work in the yard. Betsy Ann was outside helping me when Johnny pulled into our driveway, having come straight from the airport. In the next fifteen minutes, I set the hook.

After some small talk, Johnny got down to business. He asked what I'd learned, and I said the partner in charge of litigation, John Hutcherson a/k/a Hutch, had told me the firm was changing its approach to associate compensation. The partners had decided it was unfair to pay every associate in the same class the same salary when their contributions to the firm were often very different. From now on, he'd said, salaries and raises would be based on merit, not seniority. Johnny asked how they would determine merit. I said I didn't know but assumed it would be based on the quality and quantity of an associate's work. Johnny objected and said they

should have told us sooner. I remember thinking to myself, why, so you could have tried harder?

I had shared the details of my plan with Betsy Ann, and she listened intently as Johnny and I talked. As he pulled out of the driveway, the hook firmly embedded, she said she would never believe another word I said. It did go well, if I do say so myself.

The conspiracy grew. I told Hutch about our plan. I enlisted the firm's accounting department. They prepared dummy checks for Perry and me giving us generous raises. Johnny's real check would of course have no raise at all. All the pieces were in place for the big denouement.

At the appointed time on payday, Perry stopped by Johnny's office, told him I'd found out more, and they came immediately to mine. As they closed the door and sat down, I surreptitiously hit the record button on my cassette player. I wanted to preserve the conversation for posterity.

They sat beside each other across the desk from me. Johnny leaned in expectantly. Perry was struggling to keep a straight face and leaned out so Johnny couldn't see him. I shared the fake good news and the fake bad. Hutch had told me, I claimed, that the raises ranged from $9,000 on the high end, which was much higher than was customary, to nothing at all on the low. Johnny was incredulous. How could someone get no raise at all? They must have decided some of the associates didn't deserve one, I said.

My secretary Melissa, another co-conspirator, called and asked if it was time. I said yes and hung up. Seconds later there was a knock on the door. Caroline Shelby of the firm's accounting department was walking around the office distributing paychecks. That's really how we did it back then. Direct deposit was not yet a thing. She saw Johnny and Perry in my office, feigned surprise, and offered to come back later. That wouldn't be necessary, I said, and she handed us our checks.

I watched as Johnny stared at his. Five seconds passed in silence. Then I posed a question to the two of them: "How'd you do?" Perry said he thought he'd done well. He asked for my calculator so he could multiply the gross amount of his check by twenty-four to determine his annual salary. He punched the buttons and announced his raise was $8500. I congratulated him. Johnny said nothing. He continued to stare at his check.

Perry handed the calculator back to me, and I multiplied the gross amount of my check by twenty-four. I already knew the answer; I had given myself an $8000 raise. I shared the good news, and Perry returned my congratulations. Johnny was still silent, still staring.

After a few seconds, he spoke for the first time. "Give me that calculator." He didn't say please. Why he would need a calculator when his salary was unchanged was a mystery to me, but I handed it over. He did the calculation. No doubt hoping he'd made a mistake, he did it again. I asked him the result. To his credit, he told the truth.

"I didn't get a raise."

"Nothing?" I asked.

"Nothing," he answered.

"Really?" I asked.

"Really," he answered.

Perry and I offered our sympathy and said it was unfair. Terribly unfair. Johnny was going through the five stages of grief. Calculators don't lie, so he segued from denial to anger. He jumped to his feet and reached for the door. "This is BS. I'll see what Hutch has to say about this."

I couldn't control what might happen in a confrontation between Johnny and the chair of litigation and decided it was time to pull the plug. As Johnny reached to open the door, I called his name. He turned and looked at me. I smiled and said, "We screwed you." He sat back down, and we explained the whole thing. Johnny's a good sport and was a good sport even then, and he was probably too relieved to be angry. He shook our hands and congratulated us on a job well done.

When I talked to Hutch later, I was grateful I pulled the plug when I did. If Johnny had come to see him, he was planning to tell Johnny what we'd done and turn the joke on us. They would have either staged a fight in the hall, or Johnny would have left the office and disappeared for several hours. Either plan would have left Perry and me in worse shape than not getting a raise.

We soon learned what our raises were. They were, once again, based entirely on seniority. Johnny, Rod, and I were invited to become partners in the firm a year later, Perry a year after that. Regrettably, the recording of the conversation got lost somewhere along the way.

My Friend John

Here's another trigger warning: If you want to stick with amusing stories, skip this one. There's nothing amusing about it. I guess I could have skipped it too, but it's too important to my life in the law to leave out.

John Hutcherson was a gentleman and a scholar, my friend and my mentor. He grew up in Oxford, played football at Yale, and served in the Navy. He then went to law school at UVA, returned to Mississippi, and joined the Brunini firm. By the time I met him, he was an accomplished litigator in his early forties. I enjoyed his company immensely and learned immeasurably from working with him.

After I transferred to the litigation department, John chose me to be his right-hand man. I worked on all his cases, including major contract disputes, securities fraud cases, and nursing home patient liability claims. I learned more from him about how to handle a case than from any other lawyer, even more than I learned from Judge Clark. John and I worked together constantly for the last five years of his life.

John had a Type A personality and great self-discipline. He sat at his desk in a straight-backed wooden chair with no cushion and edited documents with red pencils that had to be sharp. He wasn't one to toss around compliments. His compliments to me were having me work on his cases, asking my opinion, and treating me as a peer. Though he was rail thin, ate a healthy diet, and worked out religiously, John suffered from heart disease. He had open-heart surgery even before I met him.

John and I defended Beverly Enterprises in eighteen cases alleging patient abuse and neglect at a Beverly nursing home in

McComb, a small town eighty miles south of Jackson. We hated the cases. The subject matter was depressing and difficult. In some cases, families complained that the staff restrained the residents, in others that the residents fell because the staff failed to restrain them. We litigated the causes of bedsores and residents' deaths. The deaths were predictable. It's sad to say, but the elderly are sent to nursing homes to die. The average life expectancy after a person is admitted to one is only two years.

Lawsuits alleging nursing home residents received poor care are difficult to defend. Employee turnover is high and, by the time a suit is filed, the aides and orderlies who cared for the resident are often long gone and no longer around to explain their actions. Records documenting the care are often sloppy and incomplete. And sometimes the care residents receive really is poor. Most staff members care about their patients and do their best, but there are exceptions, and maintaining adequate staffing levels is a constant challenge.

The lawyers on the other side also made us hate the nursing home cases. I had good relationships with most of the lawyers I litigated against in my career and became close friends with several, but John and I could not get along with the plaintiffs' lawyers in the McComb cases. They were chronically late for depositions and never apologized. They didn't honor commitments. One of them, a former college football player, threatened to "screw [my] little ass into the floor" in an argument over documents. John and I bemoaned the fact that he went to UVA and I went to Duke and we were now having to litigate these cases against these lawyers. We couldn't wait for them to end.

The eighteen cases were split evenly among the three federal trial judges in Jackson, William Barbour, Tom Lee, and Henry Wingate. After depositions and document discovery ended, the judges granted our motions to dismiss some of the plaintiffs' claims, but none of the cases were dismissed in their entirety. Once the motions were decided, it was time for trials to start.

We tried the first case before Judge Lee in October 1989. The named plaintiff, Ralph Felder, claimed his mother received poor care in the home before she died. Ralph loved his mother and was sympathetic, but his case was weak. His lawyers tried to overcome the flaws by introducing every available piece of evidence to paint Beverly and the home in a bad light, regardless of whether it had anything to do with the care Ralph's mother received. A trial that should have been over in two or three days lasted two weeks. We didn't win, but Ralph's victory was Pyrrhic. The jury returned a verdict of $15,000.

The plaintiffs' lawyers had the cases on a contingency and couldn't have made more than a few dollars an hour for their extensive work on the Felder case. But they licked their wounds and prepared for the next trial, which was scheduled for February 1990 before Judge Wingate. Over our objection, he consolidated two of the cases so they could be tried together.

The two cases could not have been more different. The residents, who both died years before trial, were Frederick Bolian and Margie Berryhill. Mr. Bolian's stay in the home was relatively short, and he was in the same condition when he left the facility as when he arrived. Contemporaneous records showed he enjoyed living there and cried when his son took him out. Mrs. Berryhill suffered from advanced dementia and lived in the nursing home for more than a decade before she died there. Most of the time, she had no idea where she was. A former aide claimed Mrs. Berryhill was abused and mistreated by other aides and orderlies. Her family never came to see her, and it's a known fact that nursing home residents who have frequent visitors receive better care than those who don't.

John and I divided responsibilities for the trial. He was much more experienced and took Berryhill, the much harder case. I took Bolian. Judge Wingate gave us permission to give separate opening statements. For the few witnesses who would testify in both cases, John would question them about his, then I would question them about mine.

Not long after the trial began, I could tell something was wrong with John. His eyes were bloodshot; he was listless. When I asked what was wrong, he said he wasn't sleeping well but assured me

he was going to be fine. John would never say he was going to be anything else.

But as the first week of the trial wore on, he got worse, not better. When I asked again, he said he was having heart palpitations. I knew of his heart disease and suggested we speak to Judge Wingate, who was also a Yale alum. I said the trial wasn't worth risking his health. He turned me down and continued to insist he would be fine. I should have pressed the point, but he was in charge.

The weekend break didn't help and, by the middle of the second week, the problem wasn't just John's appearance. The Type A Navy veteran had become utterly helpless. He was lead counsel but could no longer contribute to the defense of his client. He stopped questioning witnesses and presenting arguments. I took over his responsibilities in Berryhill and learned the case on the fly. With his blessing, I told Judge Wingate and the jury he was under the weather. When I said again that we should go to the judge, John no longer said he would be fine. He changed the subject from him to me and said I was doing fine.

The trial was coming to an end by the middle of the third week, but there was still a great deal of work to do. The prospect of my having to do it all must have pained John immensely. The plaintiffs' lawyers announced they would call three rebuttal witnesses, two in Berryhill and one in Bolian. I volunteered to cross-examine all three. I would also handle our motion for directed verdict, arguing that the judge should dismiss the cases without submitting them to the jury, and I would be responsible for the charge conference, when we would present arguments about the instructions on the law the judge would read to the jury.

After the charge conference, it would be time for closing arguments. John was in terrible shape, but his sense of honor and duty required him to give it his best shot. He said he would prepare and present our argument in the Berryhill case. I wondered if he could do it—he hadn't spoken a word in the courtroom in more than a week—but he was still lead counsel. It was his call.

John and I returned to the office with paralegal Debra Hammack on the evening before the last day of the trial. Debra and I worked in a conference room, where I put together an outline for my closing in Bolian while she made sure all our exhibits were in order and we had everything we might need the next day. John went downstairs to the firm's law library to work on his argument in Berryhill.

At eight o'clock, John walked back into the conference room. He was a beaten man and looked it. My friend then sat down and said one of the most pitiful things I've ever heard. He told me he was having trouble and asked me to tell him what to say. I shared my thoughts for fifteen minutes while he took notes. He seemed relieved, thanked me, and headed back downstairs.

After he left, Debra and I stared at each other. She had worked with John far longer than I had and loved him dearly. I made a prediction. I said he would be back upstairs in half an hour and tell us he couldn't do it.

It took him only twenty minutes. He said he'd tried but failed, that whatever I would say would be far better than anything he could say. I tried to make light of it, said I liked the sound of my own voice, and told him not to worry about it. He apologized for letting us down, thanked me again, and headed home. That he was unable to do what he'd excelled at doing his entire professional life must have been excruciating.

I handled everything on the last day while John sat and watched. As we expected, the judge denied our directed verdict motion. The jury reached identical verdicts of $250,000 in the two cases, half actual damages and half punitive. By today's standards, the verdicts were modest. Even more than three decades ago, the verdict in Berryhill was understandable and could have been much worse, though the result in Bolian was hard for me to accept. But my disappointment was outweighed by my relief that the trial was over. John had made it to the end and could now get the rest and medical attention he desperately needed.

The trial ended on the afternoon of Thursday, February 22, Washington's birthday. Friday was a rough day. We had to call several Beverly officials and tell them about the verdict and our plans for a post-trial motion. They had undoubtedly heard about John's situation from the company representative who attended the trial, but they had the grace not to mention it. They were receiving inquiries from the press and needed our advice about the company's response. I recently learned there was a front-page story about the trial in the *New York Times*. Why the *Times* believed a half-million-dollar verdict in Mississippi was newsworthy, I have no idea.

I took the weekend off for the first time since Christmas, and John seemed to be himself when I arrived at work on Monday. I spent the day outlining arguments for our post-trial motion and searching for cases we could cite. On Tuesday morning, I went to John's office to discuss my progress. While I was there, Leigh Allen, John's closest friend in the firm, stopped by for a visit. Leigh made small talk and didn't mention the verdict or John's health. It was a kind gesture, Leigh's way of checking on John.

The conversation dragged on, with Leigh sharing details of his golf weekend in Mobile, the names of his playing partners, the courses they played, and the outcome of their matches. John didn't play golf and cared nothing about it. When he cut his eyes toward me, I knew he was ready to get back to work. Leigh finally left, and John looked at me, smiled, and said, "What makes him think we give a tinker's damn about his golf weekend with a bunch of rich guys in Mobile?" Leigh loved talking about golf almost as much as he loved playing it. I smiled back and thought to myself, he's okay; he's going to be fine.

I later learned that John went to lunch at the Petroleum Club with a group from the firm and seemed in good spirits. He didn't come straight back to the office with them but begged off to run an errand. Before he left for the day, he stopped by the library to ask if I'd found anything new in my research. I gave him a quick overview, then he told me something that was out of character. If there was anything useful to be found, he said, he knew I would find it. The comment struck me as odd. It wasn't like him.

Around ten o'clock on Wednesday morning, word spread at the office that something was wrong with John. I was afraid it was a heart attack, but that wasn't it. We soon learned that his errand after lunch on Tuesday was to a hardware store, where he bought a rope. After stopping by the library to speak to me, he went home, treated himself to a large pizza, likely his first in years, then fashioned a noose on one end of the rope and tied the other to the banister at the top of the stairs. He then put the noose around his neck, climbed to the top of the banister, and jumped.

The housekeeper found John's body the next morning. His wife, Penny, was out of town. Poor Penny was married twice and widowed twice. Both husbands committed suicide.

In the days after John's death, I learned two things I wish I'd known earlier. The first was that John was suffering from severe depression. I researched the terrible affliction, about which I knew nothing, and read *Darkness Visible*, William Styron's memoir about his struggle with the disease. I learned that the inability to function that overcame John during the trial was a classic symptom. It creates a vicious cycle. Depression prevents a person from functioning and fulfilling his responsibilities, which leads to guilt and makes the depression worse.

I also learned what was almost certainly the principal cause of John's depression. He was part owner of a savings and loan in north Mississippi, and a change in federal regulations had left it on the verge of collapse. I knew about his interest in the S&L but not its condition. During the trial, John's devoted secretary, Cindy Lucas, was at M. D. Anderson in Houston being treated for cancer. When she returned to Jackson after his death, she said she felt guilty for not being at the office to shield him from calls about the crisis at the S&L. She couldn't blame herself, I told her.

The S&L soon failed, and a regulatory agency filed suit alleging that John had committed malpractice. The complaint named as defendants both the firm and all its partners, including those of us who'd just become partners a year earlier. I had missed out on a Caprice Classic and was now a defendant in a lawsuit in federal court. John was the only witness who could have defended us, but he was in the grave. We settled.

I wish I had known about John's depression and its cause when his suffering became obvious during the trial. I don't know what difference it would have made or if there's anything I could have done, but I wish I had done something.

That final Tuesday, before he stopped by the library to see me, John called Debra into his office, where they went through all the documents on his desk, worktable, and credenza to make sure she knew what they were and what to do with them. She thought it was odd but assumed he was just tidying up and going over his other cases after a three-week trial. But that wasn't it. John planned to hang himself in just a few hours, but first he needed to take care of his clients. To the very end, he was the consummate professional.

John died on the night of February 27, 1990. He was fifty years old.

F ocusing on work in the days after John's death was difficult, but I had no choice. The deadline for the post-trial motion was looming. After all the briefs were filed, Judge Wingate did something judges rarely do: To his credit, he admitted he'd made a mistake, that he never should have consolidated the two cases for trial. Because the inflammatory evidence about Mrs. Berryhill's treatment violated Beverly's right to a fair trial in the Bolian case, he granted a new trial in Bolian.

But there was no retrial in Bolian and no more trials in the McComb cases. Magistrate Judge John Roper, who at one time was the longest-serving federal magistrate judge in the country, excelled at convincing litigants and lawyers to settle cases. Though the McComb cases weren't assigned to him, the district judges enlisted him to conduct a settlement conference. It took two days, but he finally persuaded the parties to come to an agreement. The settlement meant the cases that were keeping me busy were over, but as far as I was concerned, it was good riddance.

But the end of the McComb cases did not mean the end of my work for Beverly. The company hired me to defend several other cases alleging poor resident care. A new in-house lawyer I'll call Dick was hired to oversee them. One was soon set for trial, again before Judge Wingate in Jackson.

The principal claim in the case was horrifying—an elderly resident was allegedly raped by an orderly shortly before her death—but the evidence supporting it was weak. The best proof was a nurse's testimony that a bruise on the resident's thigh appeared to be a bite mark.

Judge Wingate ruled in our favor on pretrial motions, finding that Beverly could not be liable even if the assault occurred unless the company was negligent in hiring, training, or supervising the orderly. The plaintiff's attorneys responded by reducing their settlement demand from $500,000 to $150,000.

Dick called me a few days before trial and said he would be unavailable when the time came. He directed me to deal with the company's risk manager, whose office was next door to his at Beverly's headquarters in Fort Smith, Arkansas.

On the morning the trial was to begin, Judge Wingate ruled in our favor on several key evidentiary issues, then suggested we discuss settlement before picking a jury. His sales pitch to the plaintiff's lawyers was simple. They would have a hard time convincing the jury that the resident was sexually assaulted or that Beverly was negligent, and they would have to do both to win. And even if they did, the verdict might not survive a post-trial motion and appeal. The judge's sales pitch to me was that Beverly might win the lawsuit battle but lose the public-relations war. In all likelihood, we would ultimately prevail in the case, but did Beverly really want to risk a jury finding that an orderly in one of its homes raped one of the elderly residents entrusted to its care?

Plaintiffs' counsel reduced their settlement demand in light of the evidentiary rulings, and we then went back and forth. They reduced their demand incrementally, and I increased our offer, each time after talking to the risk manager and securing her approval. When they came down to $40,000, I told her the cost to try the case and brief an appeal would probably be more than that, and she instructed me to agree to the $40,000. Because our motions were successful, we were able to settle for less than our expected fees and avoid the possibility of disastrous publicity. I considered it a good day's work.

But Dick disagreed, as I soon learned. Ten days later, he sent me a curt letter saying he'd been told of the favorable evidentiary rulings and was mystified that we had settled. Nor could he understand why he had not yet received a full report from me. I presumed the risk manager had briefed him on the negotiations and our thinking, and he had my phone number if he wanted to discuss the matter further. But instead of calling, Dick sent me the letter. I drafted a response detailing what happened. I omitted all the profanity I wanted to include, then watered the letter down, then watered it down some more and sent it. I heard nothing further from Dick.

But several months later, he sent me another curt letter. He was terminating the firm's representation in my two remaining cases for the company and instructed me to box up our files and send them to another firm in Jackson he'd hired. I did so gladly. Getting fired by a client was embarrassing, but litigating about alleged rapes and bedsores and getting second-guessed by a guy like Dick was no way to go through life. It was even better riddance this time.

Eight or ten years rolled by, and the firm was again contacted by a Beverly representative. An older lawyer had been engaged to assess the company's litigation strategy and selection of outside counsel, and he wanted to talk to us about defending more cases. I didn't want to return to nursing home litigation and fortunately was too busy to do so, but I was asked to attend the meeting because of my past work for the company.

Near the end, I asked the lawyer if Dick was still with Beverly. He said it was funny I should ask. Dick, he reported, was currently serving time in federal prison. His offense was soliciting bribes from law firms in exchange for sending them work. I was overcome with schadenfreude and shed nary a tear. Beverly again retained the firm, but I never worked on a nursing home case again.

That Short Little Pipeline Lawyer

One of the matters on which I was working with John when he died was a multimillion-dollar breach-of-contract case involving natural-gas prices. Our client was United Gas Pipe Line Company, which sold natural gas to an electric utility, Mississippi Power & Light. MP&L burned the gas to generate electricity for its customers.

A dramatic drop in the price of natural gas led to the lawsuit. In past years, United had entered into long-term, fixed-price contracts with producers to ensure an adequate supply to satisfy its contract with MP&L. The price United charged MP&L was based on the prices in those contracts. When MP&L observed that the current market price was much lower than the price it was paying, it sued United for the difference.

John and I weren't the only firm lawyers working on the case. David Kaufman, a fine lawyer and good friend four years my senior, handled most of the workload and took and defended most of the depositions. When John died, David became lead counsel, and I moved up from third chair to second. With the head of our team gone and the case set for trial, David and I worked feverishly to get ready. We were hard at it for twelve hours a day, seven days a week, as the trial date approached.

Overwork and undersleep can make a person goofy, and David and I had our share of goofy episodes. One was on a flight home to Jackson from United's headquarters in Houston and involved one of MP&L's key witnesses, a man named Tom.

Tom had the worst comb-over you've ever seen. He was almost completely bald but refused to accept his condition with grace. Instead, he allowed the limited remaining hair sprouting from above one ear to grow long. He wore the foot-long strands draped across the top of his head and pasted them down to keep them from escaping and flapping in the breeze like a horse's mane. Tom's purpose was to create the illusion that he had a full head of hair, but he wasn't fooling anybody. David and I were both appalled. David, who was still in his thirties but prematurely bald, was especially offended. Tom gave bald men a bad name.

We had decided David would give our opening statement and I would handle voir dire, the stage at the beginning of a trial when lawyers get to question potential jurors to determine their suitability. On the flight home from Houston, we decided I should make Tom's terrible comb-over a central theme of my questioning. I wouldn't really, but it was fun to imagine it. Becoming goofier by the minute, we took turns proposing questions I would ask the potential jurors. It went something like this:

"Deception comes in many forms, do you all agree with that?"

"And do you also agree that a man who will deceive you about one thing will deceive you about others? You've all known men like that, haven't you? If you haven't, please raise your hand. Let the record reflect that there are no hands raised. Thank you."

"If a man has engaged in deceptive conduct, you would want to know that in evaluating his testimony at trial, wouldn't you?"

"Because he might be trying to deceive you too, isn't that right? Anyone disagree? Nobody? Good."

"When I use the term comb-over, do you all know what I mean by that?"

"Some of you don't look so sure, so let me tell you. A comb-over, which is sometimes called a dome wrap, is when a bald-headed man grows the little bit of hair he has left real long and combs it over the top of his head to the other side. That gives him hair on top of his head even though it's not growing out of the top of his head. Some of you are smiling. You know what I mean, don't you? You've seen comb-overs, haven't you?"

"I see that some of you men, like my colleague Mr. Kaufman, have lost a good bit of your hair. But to your credit, you don't have comb-overs. Would you ever consider having one? None of you? Good for you."

"Does anybody know what the purpose of a comb-over is? No volunteers? Let me tell you what I think it is, and you tell me if you disagree. The purpose in having a comb-over, in my opinion, is for a man to create the false impression that he's not bald, that he actually has a full head of hair. Anybody disagree? Raise your hand in the air if you do. Again, let the record reflect that there are no hands in the air."

"Then we agree that a man who has a comb-over is being deceptive. He's trying to convince people of something that's not true, that he's not bald. Raise your hand if you disagree with that. No hands again. I didn't think there would be. Why else would a man have a comb-over?"

"So let's summarize. We've agreed that a man who deceives you about one thing will try to deceive you about others, and we've agreed that a man with a comb-over is trying to deceive you about one thing. Anybody disagree with that? No? I didn't think anybody would."

"Let me ask you one more question, then we can move on to something else. One of MP&L's key witnesses is a man named Tom. His testimony will be crucial to MP&L's case. Without Tom, they got nothin'. When Tom testifies, will all of you promise me one thing? Just one thing? Will you promise not just to listen to what he has to say but to take a good, long look at his hair? Raise your hand if you'll promise to do that. All hands up. Thank you."

By the end, we were drawing stares from the other passengers. If we had been in a school instead of a plane, we would have been sent to the principal's office.

I didn't get a chance to question the potential jurors about Tom's comb-over or anything else because we settled the case, again with the assistance of Judge Roper, who again was brought in just for the settlement conference. The agreement included terms of the ongoing relationship between the two companies, which the judge directed the businesspeople to finalize in the coming week. We would appear again before Judge Roper, this time ninety miles south of Jackson in Hattiesburg, to put the terms of the settlement on the record. The judge had instructed the lawyers to have the business-people available if any questions arose. The MP&L representative appeared in person. The United official was on stand-by in Houston in case we needed to talk to him.

At Judge Roper's request, the MP&L representative explained the agreed-to terms, but they were different from the terms the United guy had explained to us. I, making yet another mistake, stood up and said so. I should have let David do it; he was lead counsel and should have taken the heat.

It now looked like the big settlement Judge Roper had engineered was about to crater. Not only that, but as we found out later, he had a raging toothache. I was the messenger, and he proceeded to kill me, at least verbally.

"Where is your company representative?"

"He's in Houston, Your Honor. He's standing by and available by phone. We can call him now."

"But I told you to have him here today. Why is he not here?"

"I'm sorry, Your Honor. We thought he just needed to be available by phone. We must have misunderstood."

We didn't misunderstand. The judge said our guy just needed to be available, not that he needed to fly in from Houston. But though I was dumb for standing up, I wasn't dumb enough to tell a federal judge with a toothache I was right and he was wrong. The verbal beating continued, and my morale did not improve. When it ended, we went back into chambers, called the United guy, and the misunderstanding was soon resolved. Judge Roper then told us about his toothache and apologized.

In the meantime, Johnny Wade, who was in Hattiesburg for a hearing in another matter, stopped by Judge Roper's courtroom to check on us. He stuck his head in and asked the bailiff what was going on. According to Johnny, the bailiff told him, "I don't know, but I sure wouldn't want to be that short little pipeline lawyer."

It's true that I never quite made it to 5'10", but on the plus side, I still have nearly half my hair. And here's another thing that's true: No matter how much more of my hair I lose, I swear on all that's holy that I will never have a comb-over.

She Didn't Say When

Y oung adults who grew up in big families tend to want big families. At least that's what I've observed. If they have lots of brothers and sisters, they often want lots of children. I had one sibling; Betsy Ann had three. I wanted two children; she wanted more. My role as the family's sole breadwinner and worrier about finances made me resolute on the issue. Jackson had lousy public schools and expensive private ones. When I pictured myself struggling to save for retirement while paying tuition for a whole passel of kids, I didn't like what I saw.

We had a daughter in 1984 and a son three years later. We had replaced ourselves, and I viewed our family as complete. Betsy Ann did not. When our son was eighteen months old, just as when I received the email from the woman at the Mississippi Bar thirty-five years later, it was time to fish or cut bait. We would either try to have a third child or do something to make sure we didn't. A polite debate ensued. Neither of us was aggressive, but our positions on the subject were crystal clear.

Our debate soon focused on whether Betsy Ann should get back on the pill. Her doctor had taken her off of it for some reason, but he'd recently given her the go-ahead to resume. I supported resumption; Betsy Ann did not. I wanted to recreate; she wanted to procreate.

Then one night the issue was resolved in my favor, or at least I thought it was. What brought the matter to a head was my immature behavior. I went out with some buddies, had a little too much to drink, and got home a little later than I said I would. It happens. Betsy Ann was not pleased. After chastising me, she turned to our ongoing debate. She said I was right. Because I couldn't seem to grow up, we didn't need to have any more children. She was, she declared, getting back on the pill.

I managed not to smile when she said it, but I grinned from ear to ear when we turned out the lights. Though a good deed is often met with punishment, my misconduct had been handsomely rewarded. I had fun with my friends, and Betsy Ann was getting back on the pill. It was a red-letter night.

Fast forward four months, to a Saturday morning in the early autumn of 1989. I woke up, rubbed my eyes, and shuffled to the bathroom. Betsy Ann was already in the kitchen. I spotted something on the counter. I picked it up and examined it. It was an in-home pregnancy test. I'd never seen one before. The box said a circle meant the test was positive. There was a circle, bright as the sun. Taking the test with me, I walked to the kitchen. I began the conversation with the obvious question: "Whose is this?"

After Betsy Ann confirmed that it was hers, I spent the next several minutes playing the role of good, supportive husband. I asked how she felt and how far along she was. I said I'd been reluctant to have another child, but a third would of course be wonderful. I suppressed outrage and feigned enthusiasm. After going on like that for a while, I felt I could now say what I was thinking. "This is exciting, it truly is," I said, "but I thought you told me you were getting back on the pill."

"I didn't say when." Those were her exact words, as God is my witness. You almost have to admire her chutzpah. Almost. Our third child, another boy, was born in March 1990.

Late that year, to make sure she couldn't fail to say when again, I scheduled a vasectomy. Jeffery Boyd, a childhood friend and a groomsman in our wedding more than a decade earlier, was a urologist in Brookhaven, a small town fifty miles south of Jackson. We had satisfied our annual deductible, so my hope was to be shooting blanks before New Year's Day. I called Jeffery, and he said he could work me in. Betsy Ann and I headed south early one morning in mid-December.

They gave me Demerol for the pain but didn't knock me out. Betsy Ann, who was weirdly fascinated by all things medical, stood beside Jeffery to watch him take care of business. That was the last thing in this life I ever wanted to see. I held the sports section tight to my waist to block my view of the action and told her to make sure he did it right. It didn't take long, and we were soon back on the road to Jackson, Betsy Ann at the wheel.

I was feeling fine, as fit as a fiddle, and remembered on the ride home that the Brunini firm's Christmas luncheon was about to begin. I saw no reason to miss it and could catch a ride home at the end of the day. Betsy Ann dropped me off in front of Capital Towers, and I took the elevator up to the Petroleum Club.

Demerol evidently can have delayed effects. At least it had them on me. While writing this, I googled its side effects and saw among them mood changes, confusion, and feelings of relaxation and calm. What I didn't see was amnesia. And yet I remember nothing about the luncheon or the next several hours, during which I returned to the office and purported to practice law.

As for mood changes, I was obviously in a wonderful mood at the luncheon, relaxed and calm, and I reportedly regaled my dining companions with details of the procedure I had just undergone. The subject wasn't appropriate for mealtime, or really for any time, but it wasn't my fault. It was Demerol's.

Two new paralegals we had just hired found themselves stuck beside me at the luncheon. Based on subsequent encounters with them, I believe I made a memorable first impression, albeit not a favorable one. For the next several weeks, whenever I passed them in the hall, they would cover their mouths and laugh. I didn't ask why, and they didn't say.

Ain't Got None

This incident occurred many moons ago, so many moons that customers were still allowed to smoke in restaurants. Waitresses too. David Kaufman, our partner Chris Shapley, and two of their buddies drove down to Gulf Shores, Alabama, for a golf weekend. They chose Waffle House for breakfast on Saturday morning. The hashbrowns would help absorb Friday night. The foursome slid into a booth and started talking about teams for the day's match. They didn't bother to look down at the menus.

Life, sun, and cigarettes had taken a toll. She looked older than her years. And though all work is honorable, waiting tables at Waffle House was not her dream job. It was Saturday morning, busy as always. She moved fast and was all business.

"What'll you have?" She did not introduce herself. She was holding a pen in her right hand and a pad in her left, looking down and ready to write. This was not the time for chitchat.

David volunteered to go first. He figured it was not the time for studying the menu either. "I believe I'll have the pancakes," he said.

She looked up, glaring at David over the top of her reading glasses. She was not amused. A Marlboro Light dangled from the corner of her mouth, smoke curling up alongside one cheek. She wrote nothing because there was nothing to write. She instead dropped her hands to her hips. "Mister," she declared in her smoker's rasp, "this here's the Waffle House. We ain't got no pancakes."

When Chris told the story after they returned to Jackson, David didn't take it lying down. He'd eaten pancakes at Waffle House before; he was sure of it. Chris and I were just as sure he hadn't and decided to go straight to the horse's mouth. I drafted a letter addressed to Waffle House's corporate office. Before I could mail

it, David chose to surrender rather than face the cold, hard truth. Maybe, he conceded, he'd eaten waffles at IHOP.

Bunch of BS

At the time of his death, John and I were defending a securities fraud case for a small brokerage firm owned by Baxter Brown, a pillar of the Jackson business community and a friend of many lawyers at the Brunini firm. The firm's senior litigator, George Hewes, a fine man and fine lawyer, took over as lead counsel after John died, but I did the lion's share of the work.

The suit was based on allegations that a broker who'd worked for Baxter had defrauded an elderly woman after she suffered a debilitating stroke. The plaintiff, who was the woman's daughter and conservator, alleged that the broker had traded excessively in her mother's account to generate commissions and invested in securities that were unsuitable for her.

The plaintiff also claimed the broker had forged her mother's signature on the client agreement that was executed when he joined Baxter's firm and transferred his clients' accounts to it. It was undisputed that the woman wanted her account transferred, but the forgery allegation was still important because the client agreement contained an arbitration clause. If the agreement was valid and enforceable, the securities fraud claims would be decided by three arbitrators. If not, the claims would be presented to a jury in federal court. A jury trial would be far riskier than arbitration, so we filed a motion requesting the court to send the case to arbitration.

Based on an old United States Supreme Court decision holding that whether a dispute is arbitrable must itself be arbitrated in some cases, the court granted our motion. The parties selected arbitrators, and they scheduled a hearing to decide whether the client agreement was enforceable. If we prevailed, a second hearing

would be held on the fraud claims. If we lost on enforceability, the case would return to federal court.

The plaintiff intended to call a handwriting expert to testify at the hearing that the signature on the client agreement was forged, and we needed one to counter him. The signature analysis was difficult because the woman's known genuine signatures were all from before her stroke, but the client agreement was signed after it. The signature on the agreement looked very different from her pre-stroke signatures, but was that because of her stroke or because it was forged?

Though we needed a handwriting expert, we struck out in our search to find one. We identified three with impeccable credentials, picked our favorite, and sent the client agreement and known genuine signatures to him. He analyzed them and called with his conclusions. He couldn't say for sure, but he doubted the elderly woman had signed the client agreement. We tried the other two experts. Same story. We were left with no expert on the central question the arbitrators would be deciding.

Before receiving the bad news, we had agreed with the plaintiff's attorneys that each side would be permitted to interview the other's expert before the hearing. When I called the plaintiff's lawyers to schedule a time to interview theirs and they asked about ours, I confessed that we didn't have one. They responded that the deal was off. If we didn't have an expert, I couldn't talk to theirs.

Raising the issue with the arbitrators would come with an obvious downside. They would learn we had planned to have an expert but didn't have one. But we decided they would figure that out anyway, and the interview was too important to let the matter drop. I asked for a telephone hearing, the arbitrators ruled in our favor, and I interviewed the expert. He had impressive credentials and was confident in his conclusions.

Our prospects looked bleak. Without an expert, George and I believed we had almost no chance of winning. After consulting with Baxter, the broker, and his attorney, I called plaintiff's counsel with a proposal. We would withdraw our demand for arbitration, and the case would return to federal court. It would be as if we had never sought arbitration in the first place.

We assumed the plaintiffs' lawyers would agree, but they were in a strong position and demanded more. They would agree to our proposal only if the broker signed a stipulation that he had forged the signature and Baxter's firm paid them $75,000 in attorneys' fees. The broker would never sign such a stipulation, and an award of attorneys' fees was unlikely even if we lost on enforceability. We rejected the offer, and George and I resumed our preparation.

Cross-examining the plaintiff's expert would be my responsibility, and I set about the task of teaching myself the subject of handwriting analysis. I had no choice. This was before the internet, but the Eudora Welty Library on State Street in Jackson was open for business. I spent hours there learning the subject, and I checked out the leading treatises to use in cross-examining the plaintiff's expert.

On the second day of the hearing, the plaintiff called the expert to testify. He was an experienced witness and effective on direct, but I don't think he'd ever been challenged on cross about the substance of his opinions. He did not fare well.

Crafting and conducting a successful cross-examination was my very favorite thing about trying cases, and my cross of the handwriting expert was one of my most satisfying. Everything seemed to work. When I told George and the broker's lawyer at lunch that I still had more material but could cut it short, they told me to use it all.

The cross continued to go well after lunch, but my train of thought was briefly derailed. I had just seen *Presumed Innocent*, the movie based on Scott Turow's great novel. At the beginning of the movie, the character played by Harrison Ford gives the closing argument for the prosecution in a child abuse case. His assistant, played by the gorgeous Greta Scacchi, looks on with more than professional admiration. After the jury returns a guilty verdict, they return to the office and engage in a special celebration atop a desk.

It so happened that the arbitration was during the summer, and we invited a beautiful summer clerk to attend. When I walked back to our table to get a document during my cross of the expert, I imagined that she was looking at me just like Greta had looked at Harrison. My mind departed from the arbitration, wandered to the courtroom scene in the movie, then leaped to the desktop celebration. But then I snapped out of it and got back to business.

Not long after the expert's testimony ended, we took a mid-afternoon break. I walked to the refreshments table at the front of the room, and the chair of the arbitration panel joined me. Without looking over, he whispered under his breath, "That handwriting business is a bunch of bullshit." Well, who was I to disagree with that?

The favorable opinion whispered by the lead arbitrator was a good sign but not a sure one. He was only one of three arbitrators, and his vote counted no more than those of the other two. But not long after the hearing, the arbitrators ruled that the client agreement was enforceable. We then had a week-long hearing on the securities fraud claims, after which they awarded the plaintiff $18,650.02 in damages. Don't ask me where they came up with that amount or why I remember it, but they did, and I do. Nerd or savant, take your pick. As I recall, the plaintiff was seeking more than $600,000. The award of three percent of that amount, like the verdict for Ralph Felder, was a Pyrrhic victory.

Lemonade Gusher

I was extremely busy for the first year after John's death, but when the dust finally settled, I found I had little to do. I no longer had the nursing home cases, the matters for United and Baxter were over, and the mentor I'd depended on to keep me busy was gone. I'd also reached the awkward adolescent stage of my career. I was a young partner, too old to be a research assistant but too young to have significant clients of my own. It didn't help that I had a baby face and, unlike the Waffle House waitress, looked much younger than I was. I had a wife and three children, and the lull in work made me nervous about my ability to provide for them. In the middle of the slow spell, something happened that frayed my nerves even more. I lost a jury trial I clearly should have won.

But the loss was temporary, and it came with a silver lining a mile wide. Thanks to sixteen people—a plaintiff's lawyer, six jurors, a trial judge, three appellate judges, the general counsel of the largest employer in Mississippi, a friend at Brunini, and three more appellate judges—the lemon of the jury verdict resulted in an enormous gusher of lemonade from which I drank for the rest of my career. Many of my colleagues drank from it as well.

The trial I lost was in an age discrimination suit in federal court before Judge Barbour. My client was Republic Refining, Ltd., a small natural gas refinery thirty miles southeast of Jackson. The plaintiff, Ralph Little, claimed he'd been fired because of his age. Like Ralph Felder in his suit against Beverly, this Ralph was a nice older man with a weak case. He'd lost his job when he was sixty-one, and his wife was disabled. He had sympathy on his side but very little evidence of age discrimination.

The trial was short and straightforward. In my cross of Mr. Little, he repeatedly called me son. Whether it was to emphasize that he was an older man who was out of a job or because I looked a third his age, I never knew. We gave closing arguments on the morning of the third day, and the case was submitted to the jury.

The number of jurors ordinarily seated by federal judges in civil trials was the same then as it is now. As a rule, judges seat more than the minimum of six so the trial can continue even if a juror becomes ill or unable to serve for some other reason. But there is one difference between then and now. When the Little case was tried, the extra juror or two were alternates and could deliberate only if both sides agreed to let them. Not long after the trial in the Little case, the rules were changed to eliminate the concept of alternate jurors. Now all the jurors who sit through a trial deliberate and decide the case.

But this was then, and Little's lawyers declined to let the alternate juror deliberate. When I spoke to her before she left the courthouse, she assured me we had nothing to worry about. The jury would make quick work of the case and return a defense verdict. She was absolutely sure of it.

But though she was sure, she was wrong. Facility supervisor Tom Boyd, who made the decision to discharge Little, attended the trial. Brunini associate Steve Carmody tried the case with me. After the jury began deliberations, the three of us walked across Capitol Street to the office to wait for the call from the court. Steve worked in his office while Tom and I sat in mine and tried to make small talk. Neither of us was in the mood, he wasn't much of a talker, and we soon ran out of things to say. I checked my watch, checked it again, then checked it again.

Finally, late in the afternoon, the court's deputy clerk called and summoned us to the courthouse. When we arrived, the lawyers were instructed to go into Judge Barbour's chambers. He was holding a note from the jurors. They were hopelessly deadlocked. They had tried their best but couldn't reach a verdict.

Judge Barbour said it was a simple case, and he doubted more deliberations would be fruitful. He told us he was inclined to declare a mistrial, thank the jurors for their service, and schedule the case to be tried again. That was the last thing plaintiff's counsel Jim Martin wanted. He had the case on a contingency and didn't want to have to try it twice. He pleaded with Judge Barbour to give the jury more time.

There was not yet a lemon, but Jim's plea was the first step in turning what would soon be a lemon into lemonade. If Judge Barbour had declared a mistrial, my career would have taken a much different path, but he said jurors sometimes reconsider when they have a chance to sleep on it and agreed to bring them back the next morning. He would let the jury deliberate until noon. He brought them into the courtroom and told them to return at nine a.m. His decision to let the jurors keep deliberating was the second step on my road to lemonade.

Before 9:30, the jury returned a verdict for Little of nearly $100,000. The verdict was the lemon, but it was also the third step to lemonade, though it sure didn't seem like it at the time. After licking my wounds, I filed a motion for judgment notwithstanding the verdict, arguing that no reasonable jury could have ruled as the actual jury ruled. Judge Barbour granted our motion and entered judgment in favor of Republic. That was the fourth step. It was a crucial one, but so were all the others.

Jim Martin's victory had been turned into defeat and his fee reduced to zero, but he didn't give up. He decided to pursue an appeal to the Fifth Circuit, which was the fifth step. After briefing was complete, the case was set for oral argument in New Orleans on a Monday morning. Ann Lowrey, my precocious six-year-old daughter, rode down from Jackson with me on Amtrak on Saturday. We saw the sights on Sunday, then she sat in the gallery in the grand Fifth Circuit courtroom for the argument on Monday. I suspect it's rare for a first-grader to attend oral argument in a federal appellate court, and I doubt Ann Lowrey has ever again thought I was as cool as she did then. The argument went well, and several months later I received the unanimous opinion affirming the judgment for Republic. That was the sixth step.

The seventh step involved a loss by a different defendant in a different case. The week before the decision in the Little case was published, Ingalls Shipbuilding lost a jury trial in federal court in an age discrimination case just as I had the year before. The plaintiff in the Ingalls case was an engineer named Bob McCann. At the time, federal appellate courts still issued decisions in paper form in what were called slip opinions. Shortly after the shipyard's loss in the McCann case, Ingalls general counsel Bill Powers read the slip opinion in the Little case. That was the eighth step. Bill knew my partner Larry Allison and called him to ask about me. Larry bragged on me shamelessly (ninth step), and Bill hired me to handle Ingalls' appeal to the Fifth Circuit in the McCann case (tenth step).

I did my best in briefing the appeal, but the oral argument didn't go nearly as well as it had in the Little case. One of the judges, John Minor Wisdom, seemed firmly on McCann's side. His questions to me were so hostile that I hoped he was alienating the other two judges. But when the slip opinion arrived in the mail, the ruling was again unanimous and again in my client's favor. The quarter-million-dollar verdict for McCann was reversed. The decision was the eleventh and final step in turning the lemon of the jury verdict in Little into an ocean of lemonade for me.

And just how big was the ocean? In the third of a century after I was hired to handle the appeal in the McCann case, I had the honor to serve as lead counsel in all of Ingalls' employment cases. Over the years, the shipyard's workforce grew and shrunk with the ebb and flow of work, but it was often Mississippi's largest employer and usually had more than 10,000 employees. And every year, at least a few of those employees filed lawsuits alleging employment discrimination of one kind or another. In addition to employment litigation, I also handled a number of commercial disputes for the company and worked on a grand-jury investigation with Larry Allison.

I had a list of all of my Ingalls cases at some point, but I changed law firms three times in the last two decades of my career, and the list got lost somewhere along the way. My best approximation is 275 to 280 lawsuits. I can't begin to estimate how many hours my colleagues and I spent on all the cases or how much Ingalls paid for our work, but I can say this: Never once in all those many years did Ingalls complain about a bill.

I'm guessing there are very few lawyers who can say they landed their biggest and best client by losing a jury trial, but I'm not ashamed to say that I did.

Second Bikini Girl (And A Topless One)

Bob Smith represented Bob McCann at trial and on appeal. He and I became friends during the case, learned we both loved the outdoors, and began camping, canoeing, and hiking together. I didn't tell Bill Powers about the friendship for fear he might not understand, but there was no cause for concern. Bob and I were like Ralph Wolf and Sam Sheepdog in the old Warner Brothers cartoon. We fought hard when we were on the clock but left our jobs behind when we punched out.

When the Fifth Circuit ruled for Ingalls, Bob's six-figure contingency fee evaporated, but he maintained his sense of humor. He filed a motion for rehearing, the longest of long shots, and included a different sort of cartoon with the copy he sent me. Two animals, but neither a wolf nor a sheepdog, played our roles. The drawing was of a large water bird, a heron perhaps, swallowing a frog. But the frog wasn't going down easy. Its head was in the heron's gullet, but its "hands" were around the bird's neck in a chokehold. At the bottom it said, "Don't EVER give up." Bob had written our names on the cartoon. The bird was Brooks, the frog Bob.

I showed the cartoon to one of my partners, and he gave me a similar one. It depicted a fierce raptor, talons extended, about to bring the life of a tiny mouse to a violent end. The mouse did not cower in fear like a mouse but instead met its fate like a man. It stood there, right "hand" extended, flipping the raptor off. The cartoon was entitled "Last Great Act of Defiance." I sent a copy to Bob.

The Fifth Circuit denied Bob's motion for rehearing, and he often complained as the years rolled by that I had deprived his children of their inheritance. But we kept camping and canoeing, and he finally forgave me when Ingalls hired his daughter to be the shipyard's director of compliance at a salary that exceeded the fee he lost.

I had three Ingalls cases against Bob. I won the first two. He didn't exactly win the third, a racial harassment case, but the outcome was better for him than for me. The district judge granted our motion for summary judgment, but the Fifth Circuit reversed the decision and ordered the case to go to trial. But there was no trial. Ingalls didn't settle many of my cases, but we settled that one.

The only trial Bob and I had was in a sexual harassment case. It was my first post-McCann case for Ingalls. The plaintiff, a shipyard welder named Dawn, claimed a manager in the welding department had made unwanted sexual advances. It was a case of he said/she said with no other witnesses to the alleged harassment. Bob says there was an incriminating recording. I don't recall that, but it's been thirty years. Magistrate Judge Roper tried the case without a jury.

But first we took depositions of the two principal witnesses. I deposed Dawn on a Tuesday morning; Bob deposed the alleged harasser after lunch. I remember nothing of their testimony, but I have a vivid memory from that day. When I walked into the conference room, one of the most beautiful women I'd ever seen was sitting at the end of the table. She had big brown eyes, shimmering dark hair, perfect olive skin, and a smile that would strike a man dumb. And that was all before she stood up.

The ravishing beauty was the court reporter, not the welder, though Dawn was more attractive than most women who weld for a living at the shipyard. In the morning deposition, I struggled to focus on my questions and Dawn's answers, especially when the subject turned to her juicier allegations. After lunch, to keep my mind from wandering while Bob did the questioning, I didn't take my eyes off the witness. On my drive home to Jackson that evening, visions of something other than sugar plums danced in my head.

When I returned to the office the next morning, a new associate named John Giddens was in the library. He'd just started that week and asked where I was when he was given a tour of the office. When I told him about the depositions and the gorgeous court reporter, he asked me her name. I told him, and he responded with a startling revelation. "I believe she was in *Playboy*," he said.

I caught my breath. "You're kidding," I said.

"Am not," he answered. "I think she was in it the last time they had an issue with girls of the Southeastern Conference," he answered.

Well, this added a whole new dimension to the visions in my head. I told John he was a brand-new lawyer, and there's no way he'd been entrusted to do anything of importance. Whatever it was, it could wait. Finding out whether the court reporter was in *Playboy* was now his top priority. He nodded and said he was on it.

I stopped by a friend's office that afternoon for a visit. Knowing him well, I knew he would appreciate a report on the events of the last two days. I told him about the depositions, the court reporter, the revelation about *Playboy*, and the assignment I'd given John. He responded with a one-word question: "When?"

I misunderstood and said, "Yesterday. The depositions were yesterday."

He clarified: "No, when does he think she was in *Playboy*?"

"I don't know," I said. "Whenever they had the last issue with girls from the SEC."

My colleague, whose name I'm omitting because his wife might not understand, then did something that surprised me. He spun around in his chair and turned his back to me. Then he leaned over and opened the door to his credenza. After a few seconds, he found the object of his search and spun back around. It was not just *an* issue of *Playboy*, it was *the* issue of *Playboy*, the one containing beautiful, semi-clad girls from all the universities in the Southeastern Conference. Quite pleased with himself, he plopped it down on his desk. We opened it, found the page, and there she was. My dancing visions did the rumba.

Nearly a decade later, my friend left the firm to pursue other opportunities. While cleaning out his credenza, he came across the issue of *Playboy* and gave it to me as a memento. It stayed in my credenza until Betsy Ann and I came across it when I left the firm to pursue other opportunities in 2005. She suggested it was time to throw it out. Arguing the point seemed unwise, so out it went.

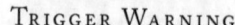

I remember two of our witnesses from the trial of Dawn's case, one good and one bad. First, the bad: Dawn had gone to a doctor with no advanced psychiatric training. Based on nothing more than a ten-question Q&A, he had not only diagnosed her with clinical depression purportedly caused by the alleged harassment, but he had also put her on a month-long medical leave. We retained a local psychiatrist as an expert witness to rebut the doctor's testimony. The shrink told us Dawn's doctor was a quack and his diagnosis was a joke.

The expert was important to our defense, but he folded like a wet tent at trial. The quack doctor was now a respected member of the medical community. His joke diagnosis was now understandable, though our guy might have done more to confirm it. George Simmerman, an in-house lawyer at the shipyard, tried the case with me. After our worthless expert completed his testimony, George was apoplectic. I said there was nothing we could do; we had to press on.

In terms of importance, our good witness outweighed the bad one. Sammy Wells was a senior official in the welding department. One day while Dawn was on medical leave, Sammy had to leave work to attend a funeral in Vancleave, a small town north of the Coast. While he was there, he stopped at the H. P. Davis grocery store. And who should walk in while he was there? Dawn, who claimed to be too depressed to work, that's who. And what was the allegedly incapacitated Dawn wearing? A yellow bikini, that's what.

Details make a witness's testimony credible. It wasn't just any grocery store; it was H. P. Davis's grocery store. And it wasn't just any bikini; it was a yellow bikini. Judge Roper ruled against Dawn. It was my first trial victory for the shipyard.

Not Till Tuesday

I've never been big on eating dinner in restaurants by myself. After I began representing Ingalls, I often picked up fast food and ate in my room at the La Font Inn in Pascagoula (always *the* La Font, not just La Font). Those who believe business travel is glamorous never stayed at the La Font.

But I didn't always dine alone. At the office one day, David Kaufman and I realized we both had business on the Coast the following week. He would be in Biloxi; I would be in Pascagoula. We agreed to meet in the middle for dinner. I would drive west, he would drive east, and we would dine together in Ocean Springs. We settled on Germaine's, a fine restaurant on Highway 90 in what was once a beautiful home.

I headed to Ocean Springs at the appointed hour and started looking for my destination. Before long, it seemed like I'd gone too far. With my mind in its usual state of wandering, I decided I'd missed it. Being a man, I didn't want to ask for directions, but I didn't want to be late either, so I decided to stop and ask.

I was about to pull into a convenience store but then spotted a Wendy's up ahead. I could go through the drive-through, ask for directions, and not have to get out and go inside. It seemed like a good plan. When the woman came on the speaker and requested my order, I apologized, said I wanted nothing to eat, and asked if she could tell me where Germaine's was.

It was a simple enough question, but I didn't get the answer I was looking for.

"Germaine?" she asked.

"That's right," I answered.

"He not here," she said. "He don't work till Tuesday."

Intro to the Non-Border Trilogy

Let me start this chapter by repeating the trigger warning I provided in the prologue. After the case with Dawn and Bob Smith, the sexual harassment cases I defended became more graphic and explicit. Don't say you weren't warned.

Sexual harassment litigation was still something of a novelty early in my career. There have always been sexual advances in the workplace, many of them unwanted, but sexual harassment was not always against the law. But when the Supreme Court ruled in *Meritor Savings Bank v. Vinson* in 1986 that sexual harassment is sexual discrimination under Title VII, boorish conduct that had been both legal and common became illegal. Some men objected to the change. I was told that a supervisor raised his hand with a question when the first sexual harassment training was conducted at the shipyard. If he couldn't tell a woman how good she looked and couldn't put his hands on her, he asked, how was he ever gonna get laid?

Not surprisingly, the old culture was slow to catch up with the new law, and the workplace didn't change overnight. In the early days of sexual harassment litigation, many of the cases were completely lacking in subtlety. At least that was my experience, though maybe it was because I represented a shipyard, not a bank or a law firm. But whatever the reason, I defended cases with outlandish allegations that made for good stories.

Late, great novelist Cormac McCarthy wrote three terrific novels, *All the Pretty Horses*, *The Crossing*, and *Cities of the Plain*, that came to be known as The Border Trilogy. I'm no Cormac McCarthy, but I have a trilogy of my own. The Penis Trilogy consists of the next three stories.

Big George

Because I defended George Fantroy and Ingalls in three trials in federal court, this story is a trilogy within a trilogy. Big George was a large, glowering black man who worked as a foreman in the welding department. I waited out three juries with George and got to know him well. He was a staunch conservative, a devoted fan of Rush Limbaugh, and a tough, no-nonsense boss. He believed other managers pawned off their lousy employees on him because he would "run them out the gate." Whether the plaintiffs' allegations were true or were motivated by his being a harsh taskmaster, I never knew. People assume lawyers always know the facts, but they often don't, and I often didn't.

But one factor that lent credibility to the claims of the plaintiffs who charged Big George with sexual harassment was their consistency. There were two plaintiffs in the three trials, Ruby Poellnitz in the first two and Alice Mallard in the third. Like Dawn, they were welders. I got to know lots of shipyard welders in the 1990s and was grateful I wasn't one. Welding under the hot summer sun in Mississippi has got to be even worse than litigating nursing home cases for Dick.

The claims of Poellnitz and Mallard had a key detail in common. They didn't claim that George had wooed them by giving them presents or whispering sweet nothings in their ears. Instead, they alleged that George claimed he had a sweet something he could share with them: a nine-inch penis. Neither said eight or ten; it was always nine. And both said he used the same colloquial synonym for penis. But the consistency was not conclusive. The two plaintiffs were friends and co-workers, and it was possible they were also co-conspirators who fabricated the same story about Big George.

I was naturally curious about two issues: Did he make the nine-inch claim as the plaintiffs alleged? And was it true? He answered the first question with a vehement no; I didn't ask him the second.

But during a break in one of the trials, I was presented with an opportunity to find out for myself. I walked into the men's room, and there was Big George standing at a urinal. The one beside him was open. I could have used it and sneaked a peek, but what good what that have done? Even if he were a man of modest means, that would prove nothing. Men have been lying to get women into bed for millennia. Unemployed men claim they're doctors. Married men claim they're single. My grandfather claimed he was fourteen years younger than he was. And what if George sneaked a peek while I was sneaking one? The last thing I wanted was for Big George to see that I was Average Brooks. I chose a stall.

Bobby Ariatti, my best friend and the subject of my first book, *Travels with Bobby*, joined the Ingalls Law Department in 1993 and helped me try all three cases with Big George. Gerald Blessey, a fine lawyer and former Mayor of Biloxi, represented Poellnitz in the first trial with assistance from a young lawyer. This was another case of he said/she said, Poellnitz had little to corroborate her claims, and the trial went well. We were confident after closing arguments, but the jurors deadlocked, just as they did in the Little case. But this time there were no more deliberations. The trial judge, David Bramlette, declared a mistrial and set the case for a second trial only two months later. The young lawyer tried the case without Gerald the second time, the trial went even better, and the jury returned a defense verdict in short order. The Poellnitz case was over.

But Big George III, which was yet to come, was a much riskier case. Alice Mallard's sexual harassment allegations were no stronger than Poellnitz's, but she had another claim I was convinced we would lose. An employee with a Title VII claim is required to file a charge of discrimination with the Equal Employment Opportunity Commission before filing suit in federal court. After Mallard filed her charge, the EEOC sent agents from Jackson to the shipyard to investigate. On the day they were there, Big George saw Alice chatting with a male employee for several minutes and issued her a written warning for loafing. It was her third warning in ninety days, and the shipyard fired her under the terms of the collective bargaining agreement with her union. Before the EEOC agents were back in Jackson, Big George had run Alice out the gate. As for the other party to the conversation that resulted in her termination, he wasn't disciplined at all.

When Alice's lawyers filed suit, it was for both sexual harassment and retaliatory discharge. Before the trial, I met with Bill Powers and strongly encouraged settlement. We could prevail on the sexual harassment claim, but the retaliation claim was an entirely different matter, especially given the fact that it's illegal to retaliate against an employee for filing an EEOC charge even if the charge itself is baseless. I gave Bill a five-minute closing argument for Mallard on the retaliation claim. The key points were simple and undisputed. A good employee lost her decade-long career over a five-minute chat with a co-worker. Big George made the decision. It happened the very same day the EEOC was at the shipyard investigating her claim against him. The man she was chatting with got off scot-free. The reason for the different treatment was obvious.

Bill and the company's president, Jerry St. Pe', viewed settlement from a different perspective. The company had supported George's decision to issue the warning that resulted in Mallard's discharge, so the company would support him at trial. As for the employee who wasn't disciplined, he didn't report to George. He was another foreman's responsibility, so what happened to him was irrelevant. We didn't even try to settle. Bobby and I heard testimony about Big George and his alleged nine inches for the third time, and this time it came from a woman he had run out the gate.

But the trial went far better than we'd feared. The young lawyer again tried it alone, and she didn't call a witness we were afraid would corroborate Mallard's sexual harassment claim. When the jury retired to deliberate, we believed we had the upper hand. Bobby, who handled fewer witnesses than I did and had more time to watch the jurors, was convinced at least five of the seven were on our side.

Again we waited, and again the jurors failed to reach a verdict. After they reported the deadlock, the judge called the lawyers into his chambers. He wanted to give the jury an Allen charge, named for an old Supreme Court decision that authorized trial judges to give an instruction urging holdout jurors to reconsider, but he said he would give it only if both sides agreed. Mallard's lawyer immediately said yes. Like Jim Martin in the Little case, the last thing she wanted was a hung jury. Bobby wanted the judge to give the charge, but I said we needed to check with our client.

Bill Powers had attended the trial but returned to the shipyard after closing arguments. This was before cell phones, so I excused myself from the judge's chambers and called Bill on the pay phone in the hall. He said jurors tend to focus more on sympathy and less on the evidence the longer they deliberate. After my experience in the Little case, I couldn't disagree. Bill instructed me to object to the Allen charge.

The judge became visibly angry when I told him our position. "Just who is this client you had to call?" he asked.

"Bill Powers," I said. "He's the general counsel."

The judge asked another question. "Is he that son of a bitch who sits behind the rail and does nothing while you and Bobby do all the work?"

Before I could answer, Bobby chimed in. "That's the one, Judge."

The judge said he didn't care what the son of a bitch behind the rail thought. He put his robe back on, we went back into the courtroom, and he gave the Allen charge.

The jury resumed deliberations and soon came up with an odd compromise. They ordered the shipyard to reinstate Mallard but awarded her neither back pay for the eighteen months since she was fired nor any other damages. It was a better result than I would have thought possible at the beginning of the trial, but it wasn't good enough for the man behind the rail. After we discussed our options, Bill instructed me to file a motion for a new trial. Finding that the verdict was irreconcilable, the judge granted our motion. The jurors could have awarded both reinstatement and back pay or neither, but awarding one but not the other was impermissible. The case had to be tried again.

It was déjà vu all over again as Bobby and I geared up again, but there was no Big George IV. Yet another female employee filed an internal complaint accusing George of sexual harassment, and this time there was a witness. The shipyard demoted George, and he vowed he would neither attend the upcoming trial nor testify in it. We could have subpoenaed him and required him to testify, but who knows what he would have said on the stand? Even Bill now viewed the situation as hopeless. We settled with Mallard for a modest amount and a promise that she would never work at the shipyard again. The woman who filed the internal complaint didn't follow through with a lawsuit, and I never saw Big George again.

Ｍy work for the shipyard led to work for other companies, some that were affiliates of Ingalls. I handled two memorable cases for Litton Data Systems, an Ingalls sister company that owned a facility in Ocean Springs. One was a racial discrimination suit filed by a former human resources manager who allegedly made inappropriate sexual comments to women at the facility. The company investigated the matter, found him guilty of sexual harassment, and fired him.

When I interviewed the women at the facility, they confirmed that the manager told dirty jokes and talked about sex. But sexual harassment requires the conduct to be unwanted, and nearly all the plaintiff's conduct didn't qualify. Most of the women to whom he made the comments admitted they were not offended in the least. Some said they gave as good as they got. One appeared for her interview wearing skin-tight jeans and a revealing tee shirt. She laughed at the notion that she was bothered by anything the manager said and told me she had said far worse. I knew she would be a less-than-ideal witness when I saw these words on the front of her shirt: "The Objects Under This Shirt Are Larger Than They Appear."

But the question was whether the manager was fired because of his race, not whether his conduct rose to the level of sexual harassment under the law. There was no evidence that race had anything to do with his termination, and the court granted our motion for summary judgment.

Walter Gex, a fine judge with a great sense of humor, presided in my other case for the company. The plaintiff, a woman I'll call Rachel, alleged that her manager, a man I'll call Dale, demanded sex from her and fired her when she refused. As for Dale, he forth-rightly admitted he had a relationship with Rachel but insisted it was fully consensual. He also denied ever retaliating against her.

Other witnesses lent credence to Dale's contention that Rachel was a willing participant in their relationship. French diplomat Charles-Maurice de Talleyrand-Perigord once said of a woman, "In order to avoid being called a flirt, she always yielded easily." We learned in our interviews that Rachel took great pleasure in the company of men and had an insatiable appetite for them. She was no flirt, though in her encounters it was the men who did the yielding.

I tried the case in federal court in Biloxi with Brunini associate Steve Allen. Things went poorly for Rachel from the start. Co-workers detailed the many deficiencies in her job performance. Her psychiatrist spoke about her emotional problems, but he proved to be little more than a pill pusher. His practice was to speak to Rachel for only a minute or two before handing her the prescription she had come to get.

Rachel testified on what proved to be the last day of trial. She did not hold up well on cross and, during the lunch break, took more than one of the pills the doctor had prescribed. When she returned to court, she was stoned out of her mind and could not resume her testimony.

Rachel's lawyer realized he was in a deep hole and offered to settle for a modest amount. I was sure we would win and wanted to finish the trial, but it was Friday afternoon and the company's in-house lawyer and corporate representative wanted to get home to their families in California. We made a counteroffer. We wouldn't pay Rachel anything, but she could remain on the company's health insurance for two more months. She and her lawyer agreed, and the case was over. As Steve and I were leaving, one of the jurors flagged us down in the parking lot. She asked if she could report the psychiatrist to the medical licensing board. I said I didn't see why not.

So, you may be asking yourself, why is TRIGGER the title of this chapter? And why is this story part of the penis trilogy? It's because of a woman whose name was Sonya and a man I never met whose name I don't remember. As for Trigger, you may remember that was the name of Roy Rogers' famous horse. I could have gone with a different famous horse, maybe Secretariat, but I chose Trigger because it's in the title of the book.

Sonya and Rachel were co-workers and close friends but then had a falling out. Sonya testified for us at trial and described Rachel's ravenous appetite for men, including Dale. Sonya also spoke of Rachel's relentless pursuit of another man, the one whose name I can't remember. Rachel had seen a photo of him, Sonya said, and she wanted him bad. Sleeping with him became her mission in life. When Rachel's lawyer cross-examined Sonya, he became fixated on Rachel's fixation on the man. He was incredulous and demanded to know the reason. "Just from a picture? Really? Why?"

Everyone in the courtroom already knew why. Everyone, that is, except Rachel's lawyer. But poor Sonya was reluctant to spell it out. The lawyer kept pressing, and Sonya kept bobbing and weaving. She had never testified in court before. For all she knew, she might wind up in a jail cell if she told the truth. Finally, when she realized the lawyer wasn't going to let it go, she swiveled in her chair and turned to face Judge Gex. She wanted his advice. The following may not be verbatim, but it's close.

"Can I tell him, Judge?"

"He wants to know. I don't know why he wants to know, but he does. You can tell him."

Freed from her fear by the man in charge, Sonya's demeanor changed. She turned back to face the lawyer, leaned forward toward the microphone, and declared with confidence, "He was hung like a horse."

But It's Peach

The third case in the trilogy began with enormous entertainment potential but turned out to be more sad than funny. The plaintiff, a shipyard employee I'll call Sybil, was pitiful. Like Rachel, she was obviously under the influence of drugs when it came time to testify. It was a deposition in Sybil's case, not a trial, and her drug of choice appeared to be some kind of narcotic. She could barely stay awake and struggled to answer the questions coherently.

Sybil made very serious accusations of sexual assault and harassment in her complaint, but she couldn't begin to keep her story straight, either in her deposition or elsewhere. Her EEOC charge, her complaint, her medical records, and other documents contained glaring contradictions. She claimed in one document that her supervisor raped her once. In another, it was twice. In a third, there was no mention of rape. Sybil also said she'd been exposed to a noose at the shipyard, but she told entirely different stories about where and when.

Shipyard management wanted summary judgment in the case very badly, not so much because we believed an adverse verdict was much of a risk, but because the company wanted to avoid the possibility of press coverage of Sybil's lurid allegations. Our motion was a long shot because a wealth of precedent established that a court must take the plaintiff's testimony as true in deciding a summary judgment motion. A motion may be granted only if, assuming the testimony is true, no reasonable jury could find in the plaintiff's favor. If Judge Gex assumed Sybil's most horrific allegations were true, he would have to deny our motion.

But we found a few cases holding that testimony can be so incredible that no reasonable jury could believe it. I wrote a brief that was short on law but long on all the contradictions and other evidence that made Sybil's testimony unbelievable. If the judge tried to accept her testimony as true, he would have to ask himself a question: Which version? We were delighted when Judge Gex granted our motion. Sybil's lawyers wanted no more of the case and didn't pursue an appeal.

Like the last story, you may be wondering how this one made the trilogy. And how could a case with such serious allegations possibly have any entertainment potential?

A complaint in federal court is not required to contain a comprehensive recitation of all the facts the plaintiff alleges. But detailed factual allegations are not prohibited, and lawyers often include them for tactical reasons. As I noted earlier, details make a claim credible. Lawyers may plead the facts in detail to convince a defendant the case is strong in hopes of a favorable early settlement.

Whatever the reason, Sybil's lawyer included significant details in the allegations about her supervisor's alleged misconduct. When I read the complaint, I deemed one section of it the wildest thing I'd ever seen in a federal-court pleading. I shared it with my friends at Brunini and considered auctioning off the privilege of taking Sybil's deposition to the highest bidder. When I interviewed her supervisor about the allegations, he was dumbstruck. He denied them both vehemently and credibly. But with all the details the complaint included, how could the allegations not be true? Who could make something like that up?

This is what Sybil alleged: One day at the shipyard, without her knowledge or consent, Sybil's supervisor dipped his penis into her yogurt. Then, still without her consent, he inserted his yogurt-coated penis into her mouth. That seems like a risky move to me, but I wasn't there. In any event, Sybil then protested the unpermitted intrusion, or so she alleged. The nature of the protest was not detailed in the complaint, but the supervisor's response was. According to Sybil, he reacted to her protest with one of his own, saying, "But it's peach, your favorite flavor."

A Clean, Well-Lighted Tip

Here's another story about a penis, but the one in this story was artificial, so it didn't make the trilogy.

When a lawyer prepares a witness to give a deposition, part of the drill is telling the witness not to guess. I gave the spiel hundreds of times. It goes like this: If you don't know the answer to a question, just say you don't know. If you don't remember, just say you don't remember. Whatever you do, don't guess. This is sound advice not only because you're instructing the witness to tell the truth, but also because in most cases not remembering won't hurt the witness's credibility. But not in all cases, as this story illustrates.

I had a sexual discrimination case brought by nineteen women at the shipyard. Bobby worked on this one with me too. The claims were weak and, after I deposed the plaintiffs, their lawyers lost interest. The case was dismissed, but not before Bobby and I had some fun in one of the depositions.

All the plaintiffs asserted claims for discrimination in promotions, but one, a woman I'll call Karen, claimed she was sexually harassed as well. The gist of her complaint was that the men in her welding crew had given her a sex toy for Christmas, a vibrator to be precise. She alleged that the unusual gift traumatized her and caused her to suffer severe emotional distress.

I interviewed the members of the crew, and they forthrightly admitted the vibrator allegation was true. When I asked why on Earth they had presented Karen with such an inappropriate gift, they had a rational explanation. She was always complaining that she didn't have a man or a sex life, they told me, and she said she needed both in the worst sort of way. None of the men in the crew were willing to serve as the real thing, so they gave her the next best thing for Christmas.

When Bobby and I walked into the conference room for Karen's deposition, we could see why there were no volunteers. Karen's height and circumference were roughly the same. I questioned her about her weak promotion claim, then turned to sexual harassment.

Karen was locked and loaded when I asked about the vibrator. Instead of answering immediately, she leaned down, picked up a Walmart bag, and emptied the contents onto the table between us. We'd heard that her allegation was true, and now we saw that it was true. There was the vibrator as well as a container of something called sex grease, which I soon learned was also a gift from the crew. Her generous co-workers had thought of everything.

The vibrator had an unusual feature, a lighted tip. I wondered if illumination was needed when the vibrator was being used for its intended purpose. Or was it one of those multi-function tools, a sort of Swiss Army knife with both sexual and non-sexual uses? If the power went out, could you repurpose the vibrator as a flashlight and use it to find a candle?

I quizzed Karen about the circumstances of the gift as well as her reaction to receiving it. She was terribly offended, she claimed, and was appalled that her co-workers would insult her with such a degrading gift. The crew had told me a different story, insisting that Karen's only complaint was that the lighted tip wouldn't light. She'd even brought it back to the shipyard to see if they could fix it.

You will recall when the devil appeared and inspired me to play the practical joke on Johnny Wade about our salaries. I didn't need the devil this time; I had Bobby. When we took a break, he had a suggestion. I should ask Karen if she'd ever used the vibrator. It was a relevant question. After all, if she used the gift, was it truly unwanted? And was she really offended? It was a good idea, so I took him up on it.

We resumed the deposition, and I popped the question: "Let me ask you this: Have you ever used the vibrator?"

She had been on the offensive but wasn't expecting this. She hesitated. The wheels turned as she pondered what to say. After

five seconds, she settled on an answer, but it wasn't a good one. "I don't remember," she said.

I pressed her. "Wait a minute, you sued Ingalls over this vibrator that's sitting here on this table, and you just told us how offended you say you were. But now you're claiming you don't remember if you ever used it? Let me ask you again. Did you ever use the vibrator?"

Five more seconds passed, but she had her story and was sticking with it. "I don't remember," she said again.

If she was going to lie, she should have said no.

Be Prepared

My father was a legendary scoutmaster. He led the Boy Scouts of Troop 12 in Tupelo for sixty years. More than 350 young men attained the rank of Eagle under his leadership. His troop began a tradition of monthly campouts in the summer of 1951. As of this writing, they have gone on an overnight camping trip every single month for nearly seventy-three years. As I noted at the outset, *The Scoutmaster*, my most recent book, is the story of Daddy's wonderful life. There are no stories like the last four in *The Scoutmaster*.

I am, not surprisingly, an Eagle Scout myself. It would be a scandal if I weren't. Be Prepared is the Boy Scout motto, and I learned the importance of being prepared from Daddy. The practice served me well in my law practice.

The plaintiff in one of my Ingalls cases was a man named Ron. He was a very able senior manager, and his case was stronger than most of the employment cases I defended. It was one of the rare cases management wanted to settle. But settlement looked like it would be impossible. Not long before Ron's deposition, I received a demand from his lawyers. As I recall, they wanted $15 million, which was many times the amount Ingalls would ever be willing to pay. We didn't make a counteroffer.

On the morning of the deposition, Ron asked if he could say something off the record before I began questioning him, and I said sure. He said he knew he'd been mistreated, but he preferred to settle the case and avoid the delay and risk of a trial and possible appeal. I told him I thought the shipyard would be willing to entertain a reasonable proposal, but his demand didn't bode well for negotiations. "What demand?" he asked. His lawyers began to squirm.

"The $15 million demand," I answered.

He obviously knew nothing about it and said so. I showed him the letter so his lawyers couldn't deny it. His face turned red; he was steaming. They were now shrinking as well as squirming. Making the offer without his consent was unethical, but I wasn't surprised. This wasn't my first rodeo with them.

The deposition went about as I expected—some good and some bad—and we soon settled the case for less than one percent of the lawyers' unauthorized demand. The rift between client and lawyers likely helped us in negotiations. Ron probably wanted to be done with them. I did too.

So what does Ron's case have to do with the importance of being prepared? I worked hard to prepare for his deposition, but I always did that. This deposition was different and called for a unique kind of preparation. While interviewing Ron's co-workers, I was told something interesting about his behavior. Ron had a glass eye. Presumably to intimidate the others in the room, he would sometimes remove it and place it on the conference table during business meetings. I could see how that would knock someone off his stride.

But being forewarned, I wasn't going to let it knock me off mine. I was prepared with a paper towel in my pocket when I arrived for the deposition. If Ron plucked out his eye and put it on the table, I was going to pull out the paper towel, pick up the eye, drop it into my pocket, and ask my next question. There was no way Ron was going to intimidate me. But my preparation proved unnecessary. The eye stayed in its socket, and the paper towel stayed in my pocket.

The Cost Of Being Cheap

I will now illustrate the importance of being prepared with a story about a time when I wasn't. The case was also for Ingalls and also against the lawyers who represented Ron.

I'm a cheap Luddite. Anybody who knows me well will confirm it. I don't like to learn new technologies, and I sure don't like to pay for them. The two traits combined to make me one of the last lawyers in America, or at least one of the last at the Brunini firm, to get a cell phone. They were expensive, and I'd gotten along just fine without one, so why spring for a new gadget that would probably go the way of the VCR? The VCR hadn't yet gone the way of the VCR, but still. Now it's a rare eighth grader who doesn't have an iPhone, but this was then, and I procrastinated.

The case was set for trial before Judge Bramlette. We were waiting for a ruling on our motion for summary judgment, and I thought we had a good shot. Magistrate judges often handle pretrial conferences, and the pretrial in the case was set before Judge Roper on a Monday morning at 10:30. All the lawyers would have to come from out of town, one of them from five hours away. With everyone's blessing, I called Judge Roper's deputy clerk on Friday morning and asked if we could have the pretrial conference by phone. She promised to check with the judge and let me know.

A little before five, I realized I hadn't heard from her. I called and let the phone ring ten times. No answer. I hung up and called back. Ten more rings. Still no answer. They were gone for the day. I would have to head south on Monday morning before they made it to the office, which meant we wouldn't have the pretrial conference by phone. Or so I thought.

I left home at 7:15 Monday morning. The drive down was

uneventful until I ran into a torrential thunderstorm north of the Coast. It was a gully-washer, a frog-strangler. Traffic slowed to a crawl. I worried I would be late.

Until after I passed my sixtieth birthday, I was a diehard manual-transmission man, and I was a long way from sixty then. I stopped at a red light on Highway 49 in Lyman, just north of Gulfport. When the light turned green, I lifted my left foot from the clutch to proceed on my way. But the clutch remained flat on the floorboard, I didn't proceed, and I was now blocking traffic on a four-lane highway in a driving rainstorm. I cursed the car and the heavens, shifted into neutral, then hopped out and pushed my car off the side of the road. A good Samaritan stopped to help. I was as wet as a fish, but he told me to climb in and dropped me off at a convenience store down the road.

I explained my predicament to the cashier, another good Samaritan, and she kindly offered me the store's portable phone so I could call the court. I explained my predicament to Judge Roper's deputy clerk, who should have been feeling guilty for not calling me back on Friday, and she said the judge wanted to speak to me. I told him what had happened and where I was, and he recommended a good mechanic who could fix my car. He said they'd tried to call first thing to tell me we could have the pretrial conference by phone, but my secretary said I'd already left town. When they suggested she call and tell me to turn around, she said I didn't have a cell phone. I could tell from his tone he found that hard to believe.

Half an hour later, Judge Roper conducted the pretrial conference at the appointed time. I participated on the store's phone from the snack aisle, rode in the cab of the wrecker to the mechanic's shop, waited while he fixed my car, then headed north toward home. (Note the Willie Morris allusion.) Two days later, Judge Bramlette granted our summary judgment motion. I bought my first cell phone the next day.

An Enjoyable Visit

I had five or six Ingalls cases against Ron's lawyers. I settled the one with Ron, and the court granted our summary judgment motions in all but one of the others, including the one that led to my cell-phone purchase. I tried my last case against them.

One of Ron's lawyers was tolerable, but the other one, whom I'll call Dick, possessed in the highest degree every bad trait a lawyer can have. Dealing with him was almost uniformly unpleasant. Trying the case against him was unpleasant and exasperating at times but fun at others.

The trial was in a sexual harassment case. The plaintiff was a woman I'll call Debbie, the alleged harasser a shipyard manager named Robert Whittington. An individual ordinarily can't be liable under Title VII, but Dick and his colleague had sued Robert individually for assault and battery. The alleged assault consisted entirely of squeezing Debbie's finger. Seriously.

I represented both Ingalls and Robert and took an immediate liking to him. He had started his career at the shipyard when he was seventeen and had risen through the ranks to become a general superintendent, six levels above where he began. He never attended a day of college but was the kind of guy who could solve any problem and build anything, who could walk into a junkyard wearing a tool belt and ride out in the tank he built from stuff he found. He would have survived on *Survivor*.

Robert was also able to read people. The night before the trial, we went over the parties' witness lists. He told me how each of them would do, and he was right about them all. He said his boss would do fine, but we couldn't count on his boss's boss, a vice-president, who wanted to please everybody. He pegged them both to a tee.

When the trial began, I found that Robert was also a great witness, though he'd never been one before. When Dick cross-examined him, it was a complete mismatch. Robert explained the facts and made eye contact with Dick, the judge, and the jury. He admitted grabbing Debbie's finger but said he didn't squeeze it hard enough to hurt. When Dick pressed him on the point, Robert invited him to walk over to the witness stand to show him. Dick stayed put. Witnesses are like relatives—you can't pick 'em—and I had many lousy ones over the years. But Robert was a natural. I sat back and enjoyed his performance. I don't believe I objected a single time.

Robert and our other witnesses took one look at Debbie in the courtroom and said she appeared to have experienced a religious conversion. At the shipyard, they said, she wore short skirts, sat atop men's desks, and made every effort to use her assets to her advantage. Now she had her hair up in a bun and was dressed like a schoolmarm. Dick played a tape Debbie had secretly made of a conversation with Robert. It didn't help her case. Robert was friendly but said nothing incriminating. Debbie sounded like a Mount Pilot party girl ready for fun and nothing like the solemn woman on the witness stand.

I also had another great witness on my side. Dorothy Myles Shaw worked at the shipyard for more than half a century, was a key witness in many of my cases, and became a dear friend. She held several positions during her long career, but she was right where I needed her in the 1990s, working in Human Resources investigating internal complaints of discrimination and harassment. She was thorough and professional and did an outstanding job documenting her findings and explaining them to juries. And she never got rattled on cross. Word got back to me after one trial that Judge Bramlette said Dorothy was the best witness he'd ever seen in his courtroom. She stuck to her guns again in this trial, and Dick was outgunned again.

Thanks primarily to Dick's antics, the trial lasted five days, far longer than it should have. By Friday morning, I believed a defense verdict was likely. My confidence rose still further when a woman on the jury offered me a homemade donut as the two of us walked into the courthouse. I thanked her but said I better not.

Judge Gex, who no doubt wanted to be done with Dick just as much as Ron had, called us into chambers to discuss closing arguments. He wanted to know how long we needed and suggested twenty minutes a side. I said that would be fine, but Dick objected strenuously. He needed forty-five, he said. Judge Gex looked disgusted but didn't want to give Dick an argument he could use on appeal. We settled on forty.

Inexplicably, Dick spent the first half of his closing argument talking about an entirely different case, one in which he represented his brother. He went on and on about it, and I couldn't understand why. From the looks on the jurors' faces, they couldn't understand either. I could have objected, but I preferred to let Dick waste his time. When I looked at Judge Gex, he was looking at me. He probably wanted me to object so he could tell Dick to stick to this case.

As Dick droned on, I picked up a pad of post-its, wrote a note on the top one, and pushed the pad over to Dorothy. She read it, got tickled and, as sometimes happens, could not get untickled. She tried to compose herself and covered her face. I had written but one sentence: "I plan to confine my remarks to this case."

All the superintendents who reported to Robert came to hear closing arguments and wait for the verdict. They clearly loved him. After the jury ruled in our favor, the five of them, along with Robert and me, went to the bar in the Bombay Bicycle Club to celebrate with a beer. The first six of us ordered Budweiser or Bud Light—this was before craft beers were a thing—but the last guy asked for Old Milwaukee. I said I'd never known anybody with a choice to choose Old Milwaukee. His buddies liked that.

Robert and I were regulars in the bar during the week. We met there every afternoon to have a couple of beers and go over what happened that day and what to expect the next. On the evening before the first day of trial, I told Robert that Debbie's lawyers might call him as an adverse witness in her case. If they did, I said, I could present his testimony then, but I would probably wait until the plaintiff rested and call him in our case.

Dick called Robert as his first witness. It was a blunder. In the bar that evening, Robert wanted to know why I had decided not to ask him any questions. I said he was great, there was nothing to fix, and I preferred to have him testify after we heard Debbie's testimony. He then asked if that Dick guy would get to question him again. When I said he would, Robert took a sip of his beer and smiled. "Good," he said, "I kinda enjoyed visiting with him."

Beginning with the U.S.S. *Wasp*, which was commissioned in 1989, Ingalls built a class of eight enormous vessels for the United States Navy called LHDs, which stands for Landing Helicopter Dock. Seven of the eight were still in service in 2024. The mission of the LHDs is to serve as launching pads for amphibious assaults. Helicopters and landing craft aboard the ships take Marines ashore. The helicopters lift off from the deck, and a gate in the stern opens to release the landing craft into the sea.

An LHD is more than 800 feet long, weighs more than 40,000 tons, and yet it somehow floats. Each ship is staffed by a crew of more than a thousand sailors and has berthing for an assault force of nearly two thousand Marines. Describing an LHD as a city at sea is no exaggeration. While on a mission, an LHD has more residents than two-thirds of the towns and cities in Mississippi.

All but one of the LHDs are powered by closed-loop steam propulsion systems. Boilers generate superheated steam, which drives the turbines and delivers 70,000 horsepower to two propeller shafts. The massive vessels are able to reach speeds of twenty-two knots, which is twenty-five miles an hour. After passing through the turbines, the spent steam is converted back to water in huge condensers. Each condenser is equipped with more than 8,000 long copper tubes through which seawater runs. The hot steam enters the condenser from the top, condenses on the cool tubes, then drips into the bottom, from which it is pumped back to the boilers. The colder the ocean water, the more efficiently the system operates.

Each warship built by Ingalls, including the LHDs, is the product of a complex, multi-year process to which thousands of engineers and craftsmen devote their time and expertise. When construction is complete but before delivery to the Navy, the ships go through a series of comprehensive tests and trials, first alongside the dock, then at sea.

Keeping the saltwater running through the tubes and stopping it from contaminating the fresh water in the closed-loop propulsion system is essential. To detect any leakage, a salinity alarm sounds if the cooling seawater contaminates the fresh water. During dockside trials of the LHD-2, the U.S.S. *Essex*, the alarm sounded repeatedly.

An investigation was begun immediately to pinpoint the source of the contamination. The joints at one end of the copper tubes were soon identified as the culprit. The condenser was designed to allow the tubes to slide back and forth through one end plate to keep them from buckling when the condenser expanded and contracted with changes in temperature. A joint made with two fiber and two lead rings around the end of each tube was designed to allow the tubes to slide back and forth but keep seawater out. In its investigation, Ingalls found that the joints leaked.

Ingalls initially doubted the condenser could be repaired. Graham Manufacturing of Batavia, New York, forty miles east of Buffalo, had built the condenser and delivered it to the shipyard years earlier. After it was installed in the bottom of the hull, multiple decks were built above it. To remove and replace it would require Ingalls to cut a hole in the completed hull and take it out sideways.

But, fortunately, Ingalls' engineers soon figured out why the joints were leaking and devised a way to make them stop. The problem was that Graham's employees had been overzealous in the installation of the fiber and lead rings. When they tamped the rings into place, they hit them too hard, which squeezed a small section of the tubes and reduced it in diameter. During dockside trials, when the necked-down sections of the tubes slid through the rings, the joints leaked.

Ingalls' engineers and machinists came up with a fix. They designed and built simple tools that would expand the tubes to their original diameter. When the work was finished, the tubes were as good as new. The alarm no longer sounded, and the *Essex* was good to go.

But the problem had been costly to fix and delayed delivery of the *Essex* to the Navy. Ingalls demanded that Graham pay the costs. When Graham refused, Bill Powers called me. It was my first non-employment matter for the shipyard and my first shipyard case in which Ingalls would be the plaintiff.

Heavyset Gentleman

The lawsuit against Graham was challenging but fun. It was challenging primarily because I was old enough to be lead counsel in a complex commercial case but not old enough to have younger lawyers working with me. As a result, I did almost all the work myself. I analyzed all the documents and took and defended all the depositions. I was not yet accustomed to delegating, and I didn't.

The work was hard, but I liked the case and the people. I worked closely with three shipyard employees: Bobby Quinn, the purchaser responsible for buying the condenser from Graham; Dave Williams, an engineer and decorated Vietnam vet who headed the investigation and repair; and John Carlson, the in-house lawyer managing the case. I flew to Buffalo three times to take depositions, and the Ingalls crew went with me. After we finished early one day, John and I took a short road trip on which I experienced two lifetime firsts: I set foot in Canada and saw Niagara Falls.

I also liked Graham's lawyers and the Graham employees who worked on the case. Robert Boyd and Bill Patterson, both from Jackson, represented Graham. They were always professional and courteous. I don't recall a harsh word from either of them from the beginning of the case to the end, even during a trial that lasted two weeks. Two of the Graham employees I remember were Al DiPiazza and Phil Marks, a Brit. Both were pleasant and gracious.

Bobby Quinn was the most gregarious member of our team. He got along well with Graham's lawyers and witnesses, and he and I became good friends. He was not only friendly but was also, it's fair to say, a heavyset gentleman. Jolly would be a good word to describe him.

The last deposition I took on my last trip to Buffalo was of a

111

young Graham craftsman. The Ingalls team had all left to fly home by the time the deposition began. I was alone in the conference room with the witness, the court reporter, and Graham's lawyers and employees. The young man had come to Mississippi to help repair the leaky condenser and claimed he'd had an unpleasant conversation with Bobby Quinn while he was at the shipyard. He testified that Bobby said Ingalls would wind up owning Graham by the time it was all said and done. That didn't sound like something Bobby would say, so I wondered if the witness was telling the truth or had the wrong guy. To test the latter possibility, I asked him to describe Bobby.

Q: You say it was Mr. Quinn who said that. Please tell us what he looks like.

A (after hesitating): He's a heavyset gentleman.

Q (after laughter subsides): Would you go so far as to say that Mr. Quinn is fat?

Court Reporter (after waiting longer for laughter to subside): I'm not typing that.

Q: Sure you are. I'm taking this deposition. Let me repeat the question. Would you go so far as to say that Mr. Quinn is fat?

A (after more laughter and more hesitation and with a smile on his face): I would say he's a heavyset gentleman.

The Poor Bitch

I liked one member of the Graham team less than the others. He was a humorless, overly serious engineer who never gave a short answer when I deposed him. No matter how simple the question, he would go on and on. If I asked him the time, he would explain how a clock was made. He also had an odd habit of frequently interspersing "if you will" in his rambling answers. Because saying "if you will" is a request for permission, I should have said "no, I won't," but that didn't occur to me. I just let him prattle on. My mind wandered before there was blessed silence again.

I deposed the engineer in person in Buffalo and, because he did more work and Graham produced more documents, I took a short follow-up deposition by telephone shortly before trial. Bill Patterson, Bobby Quinn, and I gathered in a conference room at the Brunini firm in Jackson for the deposition. The witness was in his office at Graham's facility in Batavia.

The leopard did not change his spots between depositions. On and on he went, apropos of nothing. To entertain myself during one of his interminable answers, I began scribbling on a cocktail napkin. I finished writing before he finished talking. Bobby read what was on the napkin and started laughing, and Bill grabbed the napkin, read it, and laughed too. All the while, the witness droned on. This is what I wrote:

Q: Who is your wife?

A: My wife, if you will, is a lady I first met approximately 25 years ago when I was first taking engineering, if you will, classes at the university. And the young girl, if you will, who ultimately became my wife, was not attending the university at the time . . . .

Q: The poor bitch.

A: Who?

Bobby claimed the napkin when the deposition ended. After the trial, he had it framed and gave it to me as a memento of the case and our time together. I still have it, which is how I know what I wrote twenty-nine years before I wrote this.

But my time with the jabbering engineer did not end with the deposition. We tried the case to a jury in federal court in front of Judge Gex in Biloxi in February 1995. The engineer was Graham's corporate representative, and I called him as our first witness, just as Dick had called Robert Whittington.

My decision worked out better than Dick's. The engineer was the highlight of the first week of trial for us and better than any of our own witnesses. He also had a new mannerism that made him even worse than before. He obviously had been counseled to look at me when I asked a question, then look at the jury when he answered it. He followed the instruction to an extreme, turning forty-five degrees in his chair after each question and forty-five degrees back after each answer. He looked like a robot who had rehearsed exactly what to say and do. I should have rested our case after his testimony.

Three Hots and a Cot

After the engineer's testimony, the trial went downhill fast. Graham claimed the condenser leaked because Ingalls subjected it to temperatures that exceeded the specified maximum. When Robert Boyd asked one of our engineers to state the highest possible temperature the condenser could have experienced during dockside trials, the witness hesitated, pondering all that could have gone wrong, and said 900 degrees. He added no qualifications. There was no proof that any of the things that could have gone wrong did go wrong and no indication the condenser ever approached 900 degrees. But no matter; the witness didn't bother to mention any of that. Robert let the answer sink in and wisely sat down. I had finished questioning the witness and couldn't try to undo the damage.

Some of our other witnesses were no better. I was afraid one of them would be too combative, counseled him to keep his cool, and turned him into a spineless wimp who capitulated over and over when he was cross-examined. Our damages expert was even worse, in both form and substance. Regarding form, he displayed a nervous facial twitch on cross. The worse the questioning went for him, the faster the twitch. As for substance, we had instructed him when he was hired to do whatever was necessary to satisfy himself that the costs Ingalls sought to recover were both necessary and reasonable. When pressed on the issue, however, he said he couldn't say the costs were necessary or reasonable, that other witnesses would address the issue. We had no other witnesses to address the issue.

By Friday afternoon of the first week, our prospects looked bleak. John Carlson was busy, and Bobby Ariatti had taken over and was attending the trial. Before I headed home for the weekend, he pulled me aside and told me it was a lost cause, that I should take the weekend off and spend time with my family. I couldn't do that, but I thought he was probably right. I worked all day Saturday and most of Sunday preparing for Graham's witnesses, then returned to Biloxi late in the day with Johnny Wade and Debra Hammack, who were assisting me with the trial.

I don't remember who testified on Monday, but nothing happened to change my assessment or raise my spirits. Graham planned to call two Ingalls employees on Tuesday, and I went to the shipyard on Monday night to meet with them. Bill Powers drove me from Biloxi to Pascagoula so I could work on the way. I was working every waking minute and sleeping way too little.

One of the Ingalls employees waiting to meet with me was a man named Martin Fast, a machinist who had worked on the condenser investigation and repair. In lieu of washing his long gray hair, Martin pulled it back into a ponytail. His scruffy beard was as long as his hair and could have housed a family of field mice. The thick lenses of his glasses looked like the bottoms of two Coke bottles. He rode a Harley and was decorated with more than his fair share of ink. He was bright and able and could have been in management, but management was not his style. Martin was no fan of The Man.

When we started talking, Martin pulled out his pocket calendar and showed me the dates he spent working on the condenser repair. The calendar was covered with handwritten notes, both numbers and letters. The numbers were the hours of overtime he worked each day, and the letters, WTL and WTB, signified that he worked through lunch or worked through his break. The two of us, both working men but in very different lines of work, then had a frank exchange.

"Why did you keep up with it like that?"

"Because I don't trust 'em to pay me what they owe me, that's why. I keep records to make sure I get paid for every hour I work."

"I like to get paid for every hour I work too."

Martin paused a few seconds before speaking again. He was studying me. "You've been working hard, haven't you?"

"Nonstop, Martin. Every minute."

He paused again, longer than the first time, and tugged at his beard. He seemed like he wanted to say something but wasn't sure if he should. He made the call and opted to say it. "You look like shit, man."

I stared back at the man who was staring at me. My first thought: How could anyone who looked like this guy criticize my appearance? "Oh, yeah," I was tempted to say, "when's the last time you looked in the mirror?"

But I said nothing of the sort. The last thing I needed was to insult Martin and turn yet another witness into yet another disaster. I also figured his assessment was offered in sympathy, not as a comment on my looks. And I figured he was right. I hadn't looked in the mirror, but I was running on fumes.

On Tuesday morning, I was presented with a faux offer that, had it been real, would have put me out of my misery and allowed me to catch up on my sleep. Before the jurors came into the courtroom, Judge Gex said the trial wouldn't start at the usual time on Thursday morning because he had criminal sentencings scheduled then. When I asked if that meant we didn't need to show up until after lunch, he said I could show up before then, but he might sentence me along with the rest of the criminals. "Three hots and a cot," I told him, "sound pretty good right about now."

Professor? Osbourne

But then the pendulum swung back. Over the next three days, I had as much fun as I ever had in a trial, and our prospects improved dramatically.

Martin did well on the stand and, though our witnesses had fared poorly on cross-examination, Graham's were even worse. In fairness to them, I had a wealth of facts and documents at my disposal and was extremely well prepared. I like to think I'm wiser now, but I was infinitely more energetic then. And to their credit, Graham's witnesses were honest. Unlike some I cross-examined, they didn't try to lie their way out of trouble. It's been a long time, but I recall snippets from two of their witnesses very well.

A cardinal rule for trial lawyers is not to ask a question when you don't know the answer. But things were going well, and I was feeling frisky, so I decided to break the rule with one of Graham's witnesses. A treatise on marine engineering edited by a man named Alan Osbourne was used by both sides at trial. All the engineers regarded it as authoritative, and each side quoted favorable passages. Before the cross of one of Graham's engineers, I decided to try to prove that Osbourne was a professor. I didn't know one way or the other, but I decided it would be fun to give it a try. And breaking the cardinal rule would be risk-free because there would be no downside if my effort failed. During a break, I revealed my plan to the other members of the team.

The cross went well. I had plenty of ammunition, and the witness was compliant. I came to the point in my outline where I planned to use the treatise. The next few questions and answers went something like this:

Q: You're familiar with Osbourne's treatise on marine engineering, aren't you?

A: I am.

Q: And you agree that it's recognized as one of the leading works on marine engineering?

A: I do.

Q: And the editor of the treatise was a man named Alan Osbourne, correct?

A: That's right.

Q: And Osbourne was a professor, was he not?

A: I believe he was.

Perhaps the witness knew more than I did. Perhaps Osbourne really was a professor. I didn't know then and don't know now. I sneaked a peek at the team at our table and suppressed a smile.

The other witness was an engineer from Birmingham who was hired by Graham to testify as an expert. He was a big, friendly guy and moonlighted as a high-school football referee on Friday nights in the fall. I liked him when I deposed him and feared the jury would like him too. And because this was his first time to testify as an expert, he couldn't be portrayed as a professional witness whose testimony was for sale to the highest bidder.

But at trial, his lack of experience became a major liability. He'd never been cross-examined, and it showed. I had my facts and documents ready, and he didn't put up a fight. After he capitulated on a key point, he did something I never saw any other witness do, either before then or after. He turned and looked at the lawyers who'd hired him, held his hands at shoulder level, palms up, and shrugged sheepishly. I wasn't sure if he was surrendering or apologizing or both, but I was sure I liked it.

A Verdict and a Lesson

Closing arguments were set for Friday morning of the second week. I set my alarm for five o'clock to get up and prepare. I was always better early than late. When I arrived at the courthouse at twenty till nine, I was ready to roll.

But Bill Powers wanted me to roll in a different direction. He pulled me into a room and spent the next fifteen minutes telling me what I should say. He was the client, so I listened and took notes, but I wondered how I was supposed to give an entirely different closing from the one I'd prepared. Not only that, but I didn't like some of his suggestions, which consisted primarily of ways to appeal (suck up) to the women on the jury. That, like serving in management for Martin, wasn't my style. I worked in a few of his thoughts at the last minute but not many.

After the closings, the jury retired to deliberate, and we walked to lunch at Mary Mahoney's, a beautiful old restaurant under a canopy of live oaks in Biloxi. Before our food arrived, the waiter said there was a call for me. It was Judge Gex's deputy clerk. The jury had asked for a calculator, and she wanted to know if we objected. The request was unquestionably a good sign. I said we had no objection, this time without conferring with Bill.

We returned to the courthouse and waited in the courtroom. I chatted with Graham's lawyers and witnesses. We'd made it all the way to the end as friends. At 3:30 the deputy clerk announced the jury had reached a verdict. We returned to our tables and waited, then waited some more.

The judge and jury did not come into the courtroom. Instead, the deputy clerk returned and summoned us to the judge's chambers. Judge Gex was sitting at the end of his conference table shaking his head. He said he'd been told the jury had reached a verdict but then received a note from a female juror. He handed it to us to read. It said, as I recall, "Another juror and I don't agree with the verdict, but the others just want to decide and go home." I dropped to the floor. I was still running on fumes. I wanted to go home too.

The judge directed his deputy to bring the jury into the courtroom, then robed up and took the bench. He gave the jurors a modified Allen charge, instructing them to listen carefully to each other and do their best to reach a unanimous verdict. They filed back out and, half an hour later, asked for another verdict form to replace the one they'd filled out an hour earlier. The verdict, it appeared, was changing. A few minutes later, they announced they were ready.

The total amount we sought, which our expert was supposed to testify was necessary and reasonable, was right at $2,000,000. Graham had asserted a counterclaim for maybe a tenth of that amount for the costs incurred in sending employees to the shipyard and assisting with the repair. The jury's verdict was in our favor for $1,200,000. I was more than pleased with the outcome but less than thrilled. We later learned through the grapevine that the verdict was going to be $2,000,000 until the woman objected. I guess I should have sucked up to her.

But the benefit of sucking up was not the lesson I referred to in the title of this chapter. Bill Patterson later told me they had considered not calling any witnesses in the second week of trial after our terrible first week. When it was all over, I'm sure they regretted calling some of theirs, just as I regretted calling some of ours. The lesson I learned was that less is more, that trial lawyers are usually more competent than the witnesses they question, and that it's unwise to subject an inexperienced witness to cross-examination unless the witness's testimony is crucial. The last thing we wanted was for one of our witnesses to say 900 degrees, and the last thing they wanted was for one of theirs to shrug like a sheep.

As I mentioned earlier, one thing lawyers tell witnesses before depositions is not to guess. Another is just to answer the question. Say what's needed to answer each question but no more. Don't anticipate what the next question might be and keep talking, and don't tell the lawyer everything you think he should want to know. Just answer the question. If he wants to ask you another question, he will. The reason for the advice is obvious. Witnesses who run their mouths often make mistakes and say things they later regret. They also disclose facts the lawyer would prefer to keep under wraps until a more opportune time.

I defended the depositions of many chatty witnesses, but one of them was in a class of his own, or at least I feared he would be. If there were four people in a room, ninety percent of the words came out of his mouth. He wouldn't answer any question in ten words when ten thousand would do. He made Graham's engineer seem like Marcel Marceau. The guy wouldn't shut up.

And because he wouldn't shut up, I wouldn't shut up when I gave him my just-answer-the-question spiel. I gave him tough love and said he talked too much, way too much. I told him I wanted him to give up that trait for the deposition. I instructed him to listen carefully to each question and say only what was necessary to answer it. Not another word. Not one. That, and telling the truth, were his only jobs. If he managed to succeed, I promised to buy him drinks afterward and let him do all the talking.

When we walked into the conference room, he shook hands with the lawyer who was going to depose him and immediately started making small talk. I could feel my blood pressure rising. I had seen in the Graham case that a leopard doesn't change its spots and a witness who can't shut up won't. We settled into our chairs. The court reporter asked my witness to raise his hand, he swore to tell the truth, the whole truth, and nothing but the truth, and the deposition began.

I don't remember the witness's name or where the deposition was taken. I don't know what the case was about and have no idea how it turned out. And I sure don't recall the first question and answer from many depositions. But from this one, I remember them. And when I heard them, I knew my witness was going to be a star. Here they are:

Q: Can you please tell us your full name?

A: Yes.

Sonya With a P

Katie Gilchrist is a dear friend and former colleague. She worked with me until I left the Brunini firm in 2005 and later started her own firm, Gilchrist & Donnell. She and I are currently (meaning as I type this in November 2023) coaching the high school mock trial team for the school founded and run by my daughter, Ann Lowrey Forster. Ann Lowrey's son Eason, my grandson, is one of the members of the team. How did I get to be so old?

Ingalls got sued often during my years at Brunini, and Katie worked with me on many shipyard cases. Shortly after we filed an answer in one of them, Katie got a call. As soon as she hung up, she marched directly to my office to report on it.

There was no important business reason for the call and no important business reason for Katie to tell me about it. It was just a polite introductory call from the junior lawyer for the plaintiff to the junior lawyer for the defendant. A nice thing to do to get things started off on the right foot. The two made small talk and played who you know, a practice common to Mississippians that Carrie's former boss called raking up kin. The end of their conversation was why Katie came to my office. This is how she recounted it.

"I'm bad with names. It's Sonya, right?"

"That's right, but it's Sonya with a P," said Sonya with a P.

"With a P?" asked Katie, perplexed.

"That's right," said Sonya with a P.

"Where does the P go?" asked Katie, still perplexed.

"At the beginning," explained Sonya with a P.

"So, like psychiatrist?" asked Katie, now getting it. To her credit, she didn't say like psycho or psoriasis.

"That's right," said Sonya with a P.

"I've never known anybody named Sonya with a P," said Katie to Sonya with a P.

"I've never known anybody else named Sonya with a P," said Sonya with a P.

When Katie related the conversation to me, she emphasized the unique spelling by pronouncing the silent P, inserting a short i after it, and tacking on a third syllable at the beginning. Say it the way Katie did, and you'll see why it's better that the P is silent.

Two Thousand Guesses

I'm an outdoor guy through and through. I've been one since I was a wee lad, when I spent every available hour playing in the vacant lot beside our house and exploring the creek beside the vacant lot. It's been six decades, but I haven't changed much. If the weather's nice, I want to be outside. More often than not, you can find me there, especially now that I might be retired.

When we moved into our new home in March 2020, days before the pandemic curtain came down, I hatched a plan that failed to account for the fact that I'm an outdoor guy. I placed a chair and desk in the den, where I pictured myself writing the great American novel. It's been nearly four years, but I haven't written a word at the desk. It's not that I stopped writing. I've written three books since we moved in and most of a fourth, just not at the desk.

Temperature permitting, I write on the screened porch on the front of our house. I come inside only when it's too cold or too hot. When that happens, I write on the kitchen island, which gives me a better view and better company than the den. Carrie's a magnificent cook and is usually in the kitchen now that she's retired. Our three dogs and the Count, our majestic orange tabby cat, often join us there.

The Trustmark Bank Building, home of the Brunini firm for all my years there, was a block southwest of Smith Park in downtown Jackson. The park had curving sidewalks, a pavilion, azaleas, and small, concrete tables surrounded by stools. Imbedded in the top of each table was a tile checkerboard. When the weather was nice and I could get away from the office, I would often go to Smith Park and take a draft of a brief to edit or a deposition transcript to read. I like to think I was a pioneer in working remotely, though I

wasn't all that remote. But the birds sounded better than the phone, and I enjoyed the fresh air and avoided interruptions. All but one.

Panhandlers were the only downside to working in Smith Park. They frequented the park and asked me for money. Sometimes they cited a specific need, food or bus fare, but sometimes not. I would give them the change in my pocket or a dollar or two and wish them well. I started leaving my wallet in my office so they wouldn't ask for more.

One spring morning, as I sat in the park editing a brief, I spotted someone I was sure was a panhandler. He was a middle-aged black man wearing frayed jeans. He had stains on his shirt and was carrying a tattered brown paper bag. He looked to be down on his luck. He fit the stereotype to a tee.

He approached slowly, at an angle. He seemed reluctant. I kept my head down and avoided eye contact. If I ignored him, maybe he would go away. But no such luck. "Excuse me, sir," he said. I could no longer pretend and looked up. He repeated himself. "Excuse me, sir." I said good morning and waited for the ask.

He had an ask, but it wasn't the one I expected. It wasn't even close. Had I been given a thousand guesses about what he wanted and a thousand more about what was in the bag, I would have been wrong two thousand times. He popped the question: "Do you have time for a game of chess?" To prove he was serious, he opened the paper bag to display the contents. It was filled with chess pieces. We wouldn't need a board. The top of one of the concrete tables would do just fine.

I love chess, but I was too shocked to give the right answer. I said I was busy, maybe another time. That I was busy was true, but the brief could wait. I should have put it aside and made time to play with him. I don't know what his story was, but it had to be a good one.

In the decades since that day, I've often wondered about the man I could have sworn was a panhandler. I should have taken the time to get to know him and learn his story. What brought him to Smith Park on a spring morning with a chess set in a paper bag looking for someone to play with him? I should have played a game with him and found out. Maybe two out of three, even three out of five. But I blew my chance. He repeated my last words—maybe another time—smiled, and walked away. I never saw him again.

Shooting the Clerks

I often went to law schools to interview first- and second-year students for summer clerkship positions. I had a standard spiel. I would tell them all about the firm and our summer program, describe the work they would do and how it would be assigned to them, and talk about opportunities to attend depositions, trials, and meetings with clients. I would say we had parties and other outings to give the summer clerks an opportunity to get to know all the lawyers in the firm. I would close by asking if they had any questions. Once, when I posed the final question to a student at Ole Miss, he said, "Yeah, tell me about the parties, man." He did not receive an offer.

Most of the outings during the summer were a success, but there was one notable failure. My contemporary Rod Clement was a skeet shooter, and he decided to take a group of lawyers and summer clerks to the range. Some might question the wisdom of handing firearms to young people who were unfamiliar with them, but the outing was scheduled, and off they went on a Friday afternoon.

Things went swimmingly at the beginning, but the good times didn't last. A young woman in the firm turned to speak to the others. Her gun was pointed down, as it should have been, but it was aimed toward them, as it shouldn't. There was a loud blast. Her gun had fired, presumably because she pulled the trigger.

Pellets blasted the pavement, then ricocheted in the direction of the innocent bystanders. I'm not sure how many were hit, but I believe there were three or four victims altogether, including two summer clerks. The two with the most serious wounds were a female summer clerk and my friend Wilson Carroll.

Wilson had been facing the blast, and a spray of pellets hit him in the midsection. He looked down in horror as blood soaked his jeans. He then did what any red-blooded young man would do. In severe pain, his normal stride reduced to a shuffle, he headed for a tree, took shelter behind it, and pulled his pants down to perform a self-assessment. He was, to that point, childless. Would he remain childless forever? He'd been hit with eighteen pellets, but he was still intact. I wonder if Big George would have been so fortunate. Satisfied that he would be able to carry on the family name, Wilson rejoined the group. He now has two sons and a daughter.

I don't know if an ambulance was called, but I know there was a trip to the emergency room for an extensive search-and-pellet-removal mission. When it was clear there were no life-threatening injuries, Rod realized he had to make The Call. It would be to the firm's managing partner, Holmes Adams. Holmes needed to hear it from Rod first. It couldn't wait.

Holmes was a Harvard man and a gentleman of refinement. He and his lovely wife Gail were hosting a cocktail party in their beautiful home in northeast Jackson. Someone on the wait staff answered the phone and offered to take a message. A message wouldn't do, Rod said, and Holmes was summoned. Rod cut to the chase. "Don't panic, Holmes, but we shot the clerks." To his credit, Rod used the first-person plural. He didn't single out the shooter for blame. To my credit, I have not disclosed her name, but she knows who she is.

The victims soon recovered and returned to work. At the end of the summer, it came time to decide on permanent job offers. We had fewer slots than clerks and couldn't make offers to all of them. The female shooting victim was not at the top of the list, and another candidate on the bubble had done better work. But, as one member of the recruiting committee pointed out, we didn't shoot him. I don't remember what we decided.

Jackson had a close-knit legal community, and the story of the incident at the shooting range spread almost as fast as the pellets. When recruiting season rolled around again, other firms in town had a new arrow in their quiver. "We have an excellent law practice and a great summer program," they could say, "and we promise not to shoot you."

Wherefore No More

Legalese is the bane of the legal profession, or at least one of the banes. Most legalese is archaic and meaningless, inartful and ugly. It fills time and space that could and should be devoted to substance and persuasion. Legal writing doesn't have to be stilted and boring. It can be interesting, even entertaining. And I'm certain that lawyers who write interesting briefs are more persuasive than those who load them with legalese.

And yet, since the birth of the nation, American lawyers have thoughtlessly employed legalese as a dull, ineffective tool. They've followed the lead of more experienced lawyers, who followed the lead of more experienced lawyers. They did it because that's the way it was done. I did it too when I first started out. I wasn't confident enough to know better, so I copied what I saw. But after I got my sea legs, I went on a crusade against legalese. Young lawyers who gave me drafts filled with it got them back covered with ink.

I've read too many briefs that started like this: "COMES NOW Defendant Acme Corporation (hereinafter 'Acme'), by and through its undersigned counsel of record, and files this its Motion for Summary Judgment, and in support thereof states as follows, to wit." And I've read too many briefs that ended like this: "WHEREFORE, PREMISES CONSIDERED, Defendant Acme Corporation respectfully requests the Court to grant the relief requested in this its motion for summary judgment." Yuck. A thousand times yuck.

For readers who haven't been reading legalese for four decades, I offer the following translations in brackets.

COMES NOW [Get ready, Judge, here comes Acme] Defendant Acme Corporation (hereinafter "Acme") [they're telling you Acme means Acme Corporation so you won't think Acme means

Fred or Wilma Acme], by and through [why both? because lawyers think saying things twice is twice as nice] its undersigned counsel of record [here's a shocker, Judge: Acme's lawyers in this case are the ones filing this motion], and files this its [not somebody else's] Motion for Summary Judgment, and in support thereof [not in support of something else] states as follows, to wit [why "to wit"? Because they're nitwits, that's why]. WHEREFORE, PREMISES CONSIDERED [based on all that stuff you just read, Judge], Defendant Acme Corporation respectfully [a little sucking up never hurts] requests the Court to grant the relief requested in this its [still Acme's] motion for summary judgment.

I had an employment case for the shipyard filed by a woman whose name I believe was Della Moore. I could be wrong about her name, but I'm going with it. Anyway, Della had a lawyer in district court, where we won on summary judgment. She wanted to appeal to the Fifth Circuit, but her lawyer, unwilling to throw good time and money after bad, bailed on her. Though Della was now lawyerless, she was unwilling to throw in the towel. Like Jerry Lynn Young, she pressed on. But she didn't want to represent herself, so she filed a motion asking the Fifth Circuit to appoint a lawyer to represent her for free.

Della had presumably read the pleadings filed by her lawyer in district court, and she had learned just enough legalese to be dangerous. She started out her motion in the usual fashion: "COMES NOW Appellant Della Moore." Standard legalese; so far, so good. But then she slipped off the legalese tracks. Instead of writing that she was filing "this her motion" for appointment of counsel, she wrote that she was filing "this here motion." I resisted the temptation to call it "that there motion" when I responded to it.

Big Apple Law Students Flirt with Jackson

Most of the lawyers at the Brunini firm graduated from Ole Miss or Mississippi College, the only law schools in Mississippi, but some of us went elsewhere, including Harvard, Virginia, Vanderbilt, Washington & Lee, and Duke. We had at least two lawyers who obtained advanced tax degrees from New York University, though I don't believe we ever had anyone who went to law school there. But two of our most memorable recruits were students in law school at NYU. One of them spent two summers with us, but the other one never made it to Jackson, at least not to our Jackson.

I'll write about the second one first. Johnny Wade was in charge of recruiting for the firm in the 1990s. One year in early March, a young man in his second year of law school at NYU called Johnny. I don't remember the student's name, so I'll call him Curly. Curly was one of The Three Stooges, the bald one. I picked Curly for the young man because of what he did, not because of his hair or lack of it, which I never saw.

When Curly called, he told Johnny he would be in Jackson the following week for spring break and asked if he could schedule an interview for a summer clerkship. He sounded impressive, NYU has an excellent law school, and we wouldn't have to pay to fly him to Mississippi. He and Johnny agreed on a date and time, and Johnny asked him to mail us a transcript of his grades.

A few days later, on the Monday of Curly's spring break, Johnny appeared in my office door holding a letter and wearing a smile. He handed me the letter and waited while I read it. The first two paragraphs were typical. Curly bragged on himself in the first and our firm in the second. He was impressive, and so were we. It looked like a perfect match.

But then I came to the fly in the ointment that explained Johnny's smile. After noting that he went to undergraduate school at the University of Michigan in Ann Arbor, Curly wrote that he wanted to return to the area to practice. It took me a second, but then I looked up and smiled back at Johnny. Poor Curly thought we were in Jackson, Michigan. He had gone to the trouble to contact us, schedule an interview, send us a transcript, and plan a trip, all the while thinking we were nearly a thousand miles north of where we were.

Johnny said he tried to call the number on Curly's résumé as soon as he read the letter, but there was no answer. Curly had no doubt already left the Big Apple and headed west for the northern Jackson. This was before cell phones, so there was no way to reach him now. All we could do was send him a letter, which he wouldn't receive until it was too late. I volunteered (demanded, actually) to write it. I chose to let him off easy and blamed the thousand-mile mistake on the postal service. It's been a long time, but the following is close to the exact words of the first paragraph:

Dear Curly,

By now you have undoubtedly spent a confused day wandering the streets of downtown Jackson, Michigan, in a futile search for the Trustmark Building. It just goes to show what I've always said: Those damn two-letter abbreviations for states the Postal Service came up with are a recipe for disaster.

Because Curly was a recruit, albeit an accidental one, I didn't point out that Mississippi's two-letter abbreviation is MS but there's no S in Michigan. Curly called Johnny and me after he had returned to New York and read my letter, and we had a good laugh, but he wasn't interested in reconsidering his plans and practicing law in the southern Jackson. Given the fact that Curly had scheduled an interview in the wrong city in the wrong state, we weren't disappointed.

I'll call the second NYU recruit Tim because that's his name. Unlike Curly, Tim really was interested in practicing in our Jackson, though his reasons weren't the usual.

Tim was born in Brooklyn. His ancestors came from Ireland. His dad, like many New Yorkers of Irish descent, became a fireman. Tim went to undergraduate school at NYU, then worked at an accounting firm in Manhattan for a year. He contacted us when he was in his first year of law school, also at NYU. Tim was a New Yorker to the core.

So far as I know, Tim had no family or friends below the Mason-Dixon Line. And yet he claimed he was interested in spending his life and career in Jackson, Mississippi. Why? He said he'd traveled in the South, liked the people, and loved the blues. So why not come to Mississippi, the Birthplace of the Blues? It made perfect sense to him.

It made less sense to us, but Tim was brilliant—he had a perfect score on the LSAT—so we interviewed him and made him an offer for a summer clerkship, which he promptly accepted. When his mother asked the following May why he was driving to Mississippi and not flying, he said he would need a car in Jackson. "Why don't you just take the subway?" she asked. Tim's mom was a New Yorker to the core too.

Tim had a successful summer with us. He had a delightful, quirky sense of humor, and his work product was excellent. He spent his weekends visiting blues venues around the state, and we took him to play golf several times. He was a lousy golfer, but we weren't hiring him to play on the PGA Tour. When the recruiting committee met, the decision to invite him to return the following summer was unanimous. He promptly accepted again, did fine work again, and we asked him to join us as an associate when he graduated the following May.

Tim turned us down, but it wasn't because he soured on the firm, the South, or the blues. When he called Johnny Wade to report his decision, he said he was a prisoner of student loans and had no choice. He owed big bucks and needed a big-bucks job on Wall Street so he could pay down the balance. He was caught in a financial trap that gave him the blues. But Tim asked Johnny not to forget about him. After a few years of slaving away in New York, he figured he'd be ready, willing, and able to leave his firm and return to the home of the blues.

Tim was half right. After a few years, he was ready, willing, and able to leave his firm, but he no longer wanted to move to Jackson. It wasn't that his views on us had changed. It was that a new opportunity had come his way, one that was more enticing than practicing law in New York or Jackson or any place in between.

Five or six years earlier, while Tim was in undergraduate school, his roommate decided to try his hand at stand-up comedy. Tim volunteered to write material for him, and a partnership was born. The collaboration continued while Tim was in law school, with the two working together on comedy sketches. Later, during Tim's short stint as an associate at a New York firm, they teamed up on a screenplay, with Tim working on it late at night in his office. The partners probably thought he was cranking out billable hours, but he was actually cranking out something that enabled him to leave the world of billable hours behind for good.

And just how did Tim escape from practicing law? And how has he gotten along since he did? Well, consider these facts: Tim's last name is Herlihy, his roommate was Adam Sandler, the comedy sketches they wrote were for *Saturday Night Live*, and the screenplay was for *Billy Madison*.

Tim joined *SNL* as a writer in 1994. He later became the head writer and producer and was nominated for an Emmy. He also wrote or co-wrote the screenplays for nearly every Adam Sandler film, appeared in several of them, and performed on Sandler's comedy albums. Tim wrote the book and two songs for a Broadway musical version of *The Wedding Singer*, which had a successful run of nearly 300 shows and was nominated for a Tony. According to Wikipedia, the films Tim has written and produced have grossed more than three billion dollars worldwide.

Tim was a very nice guy for the two summers I knew him. I'm sure he still is, and he's also achieved fame and fortune. Per a google search, he's worth thirty million dollars. And he's done it all by having fun and never growing up. Would that we could all be so fortunate.

But it wasn't always that way. Thanks to his student loans, Tim couldn't move to Mississippi when he graduated from law school more than three decades ago. I wonder if he looks back on those days and gives thanks that he owed so much. Just as I wound up with my biggest client by losing a jury trial, Tim wound up with a dream career by being broke.

Crowned

Back in the day, when websites didn't exist and lawyers didn't jump from firm to firm to firm, small and medium-sized firms listed all their lawyers on their stationery. I suppose there was some marginal benefit to the practice. Potential clients could see that a firm had lots of lawyers and might well have specialists who could handle all their needs. And someone skimming the list might spot a familiar name and give him a call.

But it had to be expensive. Whenever a new lawyer was hired or an old one retired, it was out with the old stationery and in with the new. And on those rare occasions when a lawyer left a firm and moved to a competitor, replacing the old letterhead had to be handled expeditiously.

I don't know how or why the practice started, though I suspect it began when firms had no more than a few lawyers and continued as they grew larger. Like COMES NOW and WHEREFORE, it was probably done that way because that's the way it was done.

Jody Varner, who's five or six years younger than I am, was one of my favorite lawyers at the Brunini firm. He's one of the two who got advanced degrees in tax from NYU, though he's not a stereotypical tax lawyer by any means. He's outgoing and gregarious and was also the firm's best golfer. He could have given Tim Herlihy two strokes a hole and taken him to the cleaners.

I stopped by Jody's office one day for a visit, and he announced that he'd come to an important conclusion. He said he'd studied all the names on our letterhead, given the matter some thought, and decided I was the biggest smartass in the firm. I knew I was a smartass, but the biggest one in the firm? I considered the matter for a few seconds, then thanked him. It was a high honor, but in all likelihood I owed the title to Adam Sandler. If Tim Herlihy had joined the firm, I wouldn't have stood a chance.

Money on the Table

I chaired one of the two litigation departments at the Brunini firm for several years. We met every few weeks to go over what the lawyers and paralegals were working on and identify who needed work and who needed help. I tried to make the meetings fun, a time for camaraderie as well as business.

As we gathered before one meeting, the talk turned to music. Steve Allen was a musician and had played in a band. He knew his music, though not quite as well as he thought he did. Someone said something about the Eagles, and Steve mentioned one of their hit songs, but he got the name wrong. He called it "Taking [sic] it Easy."

I corrected him. "'Take it Easy,'" I said.

"No," he countered, "it's 'Taking it Easy.'"

"Is not." He wasn't backing off, and neither was I.

"Sure, it is," he responded. "I'm a musician. I know."

Ah, the age-old appeal to authority. I challenged him to put his money where his mouth was. "Wanna bet?"

"Sure," he said, "how much?"

This is where I screwed up and left money on the table. I'm no musician, but I knew the song. I knew it was co-written by Jackson Browne and Glen Frey. I knew it was recorded by both JB and the Eagles. I knew it was the first song on JB's *For Everyman*, which had been one of my favorite albums for twenty-five years. I had sung along to it countless times. I knew the words, and I knew the title. "Ten thousand dollars," I said.

More than twenty people were now assembled, but the room fell silent. Nearly all of them knew I was right, but nobody spilled the beans. The ball was in Steve's court now. All eyes turned to him. Though he was a man of great self-confidence, he now engaged in a

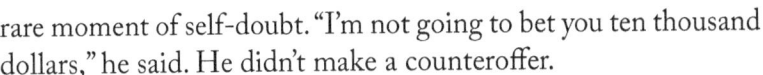

rare moment of self-doubt. "I'm not going to bet you ten thousand dollars," he said. He didn't make a counteroffer.

"Okay then," I asked, "how much?"

"Ten bucks," he said, the amount reflecting his self-doubt.

"Deal," I responded.

This was before the days of Google, so I couldn't prove I was right immediately and collect on the spot. We proceeded with the meeting and, after we adjourned, several people told me I would win the bet. I said I knew. To his credit, Steve handed me a ten-dollar bill as soon as he confirmed what the rest of us knew.

In hindsight, I never should have proposed such a large wager. The amount reflected certainty because I was certain, but I should have considered the effect it would have on Steve. I didn't want him to fold. I wanted him to call my bet and maybe even raise me. But my big bet had the opposite effect. He was out on a limb, ready for me to saw it off, but he heard me say ten thousand dollars and began crawling back toward the trunk.

I should have proposed something realistic, say a hundred dollars. Had I done that, Steve would have agreed. The amount wouldn't have been enough to shake his confidence, and his manhood wouldn't have permitted him to back down in front of his colleagues over a hundred bucks. I had a sure winner, but I should have won more. It was fun to say ten thousand dollars, but it probably cost me ninety bucks. I can't be sure I left money on the table, but I bet it did.

"Surprise?"

A Brunini colleague and I won a case because of a secret telephone conversation we were never supposed to hear. Both men on the call—the plaintiff and a key witness—agreed never to reveal it. The subject matter was so sensitive that they made a solemn commitment. No matter what, they vowed, "this conversation ain't taking place."

So how did we find out about this secret call that was never supposed to see the light of day? And how am I able to put an excerpt from it in quotes? Believe it or not, one of the men recorded the conversation and turned the tape of it over to us.

The case was a commercial dispute involving fax machines. Our client was the huge company that designed and built the machines. The model was a brand new one called the CFX-1, one of the first fax machines to retail for less than a thousand dollars. The plaintiff was a distributor and middleman in a major CFX-1 transaction. He doesn't deserve a name change, but I'll give him one and call him Stu. His lawyer, from California, doesn't deserve a name change either, but I'll call him Dick. The witness who placed the secret phone call was our client's salesman who handled the CFX-1 transaction. I'll call him Alvin.

The key facts that led to the lawsuit were some minor bugs in the CFX-1 and the means through which the machines were sold to the public. With Alvin's help, Stu persuaded Sam's Club to buy thousands of CFX-1s to stock in all its stores across the country. Unfortunately for Stu, the terms in his contract with Sam's didn't match the terms in his contract with our client. Like many retailers, Sam's offered its customers money-back returns with no questions asked. Sam's also reserved the right to return any CFX-1s returned by customers to Stu. But Stu couldn't send them back to our client, which provided warranty repairs but no money-back returns.

The consequences of the arrangement were not surprising. Many hundreds of customers returned their CFX-1s to Sam's. We never knew how many units were defective and how many were returned because of buyers' remorse. But whether a customer had a valid reason for bringing a CFX-1 back or not, Sam's took it back, refunded the purchase price, and returned it to Stu for credit. He soon had a warehouse full of slightly used fax machines and a debt to Sam's of far more than Tim Herlihy's student loans. Not surprisingly, Stu sued our client.

His first lawyer, it's fair to say, could have done a better job. The depositions he took were superficial, and he failed to plead all the claims on Stu's behalf he should have pled. We had the case won, but then things took a turn for the worse. First, Stu fired his first lawyer and hired Dick, who was an able litigator but not without faults, as you will soon see. Second, our client discovered that Alvin was involved in some sort of embezzlement scheme and fired him. Third, Dick persuaded Alvin to sign a sworn statement in support of a motion to reopen the case. In the statement, Alvin not only declared that the CFX-1 had multiple defects but also claimed he had concealed the defects in his deposition based on instructions from an unnamed attorney on our side. Fourth, the court granted Stu's motion, reopened the case, and gave him another shot. We were now in the soup. One of our key witnesses had swapped sides and accused one of the lawyers on our side of suborning perjury.

Stu's first lawyer had deposed Alvin, and now it was my turn to depose him. When I asked Alvin who had told him to lie, he identified me as the culprit. Though I knew I was innocent, it was one of the most unsettling experiences of my career. Fortunately, when I pressed Alvin about what I had supposedly said, he recanted the claim. He admitted I hadn't told him to lie and in fact had repeatedly told him to tell the truth. It's true that Alvin didn't reveal all the problems with the CFX-1 in his first deposition, but Stu's first lawyer didn't ask. Why he didn't remains a mystery to me today.

Dick's effort to discredit me by claiming I got Alvin to lie had failed, but we were still in deep trouble. The facts were complicated, but there was a significant chance the jury would conclude that the company had sold Stu thousands of fax machines knowing the bugs in the new model hadn't been worked out. Our instructions were to settle, and we had authority in the mid-seven figures.

But just as things had taken a turn for the worse, they now took an even more dramatic turn for the better. We learned that Stu had surreptitiously taped numerous conversations during the case, mostly with Alvin, and the court required Stu to turn over copies of the tapes of the talks to us. As the trial approached, we set about the task of listening to them. Cheri Green, the younger Brunini lawyer working with me, took half the tapes, and I took the other half. One morning I arrived at the office and found a post-it stuck to my chair. The message on it, in Cheri's handwriting, said, "Get coffee and come to my office. I have THE TAPE!!!"

I settled into the chair in her office and waited to hear it. The tape player was on her desk, but first she gave me the background. She'd been listening to tapes at home the night before, she said, and was brushing her teeth and getting ready for bed when the first side of a tape ended. She flipped it over and hit play, but there was nothing on it.

This is the point where Cheri became the heroine of the story and the key to our victory in the case. She would never claim she was the heroine, but she was.

Citing her admitted OCD, Cheri told me she didn't stop the silent tape after two minutes, or five, or even ten. She instead decided to listen to it all the way through, just in case. After fifteen minutes, she heard voices. One person on the call was Stu, the other one Alvin. After listening to what they had to say, she wanted to call me but decided it was too late. She instead contented herself with rewinding the tape and listening to it again, then hopping up and down on her bed. After rewinding the tape a second time so it would be ready, she tried with little success to sleep.

After that drum roll, Cheri hit play again, and together we listened to the conversation we weren't supposed to hear. It was the third time for her, the first for me. The timing of the conversation soon became obvious. It took place shortly after our client fired Alvin but before he signed the statement declaring that the CFX-1 was defective and falsely claiming that a lawyer told him to conceal the defects. At the time of the call, Alvin was out of a job and desperate for money, and he had something he wanted to sell. He would provide sworn testimony against our client, but he wouldn't do it for free.

We listened as Stu jumped at the chance to pay him for it. And it wasn't just Stu. He said he'd already talked to Dick about paying Alvin and gotten his approval. They had sued our client for twenty million dollars, were looking at a huge payday, and would be more than willing to share what they recovered with Alvin. According to Stu, Dick had said they could pay Alvin whatever he wanted and claim it was for mowing the yard or putting stamps on envelopes. It didn't matter.

Stu knew they were up to no good and cautioned Alvin about the need for secrecy. Two or three times, he said, "Listen, no matter what, this conversation ain't taking place." But not only did the conversation take place, but Stu recorded it, and Cheri and I were now listening to it.

I'd dealt with unethical lawyers and lying plaintiffs in the past, but I'd sure never had a plaintiff who bribed a witness, implicated his lawyer in the illegal scheme, and recorded the whole thing. We had to do something, but first we had to figure out what that would be. Our research revealed that both Stu and Alvin, perhaps Dick as well, were guilty of violating several federal criminal statutes. We decided we needed to report the matter to the U.S. Attorney.

We also had to decide what to do in our case. We were certain Stu and Dick didn't know we had the conversation. If Stu was willing to bribe a witness, he undoubtedly would have also been willing to destroy the evidence of the bribe. There was only one explanation. Before producing the tapes to us, unlike Cheri with her OCD, neither Stu nor Dick had listened all the way through to the side of the tape that appeared to contain nothing.

Because Stu had just produced the tapes, I had the opportunity to depose him again before the trial, which was scheduled to begin in a few weeks. Our client's in-house counsel Pat Barrett, a fine lawyer who became a good friend during the lawsuit, flew down from company headquarters. We also scheduled a time on the day of the deposition to meet with Tom Lee, the federal judge assigned to the case. Because we were on the eve of trial, we decided we needed to let him know about the startling development right away.

I made no mention of the tape and didn't play it in the deposition, but I asked enough questions to establish beyond a shadow of a doubt that Stu was guilty of violating yet another criminal law, the perjury statute. He denied that any witness had asked to be compensated for testifying and swore that he'd never agreed to pay any witness. When Pat, Cheri, and I were comfortable that there was no wiggle room, I declared that we were taking a break and told Dick we were scheduled to meet with Judge Lee. When he asked why, I said he would find out when we got there. Six of us—Stu, Dick, Pat, Cheri, the court reporter, and I—walked across Capitol Street to the courthouse. We had called ahead so we could bring the tape recorder through the metal detector.

We met with Judge Lee and one of his law clerks, and I explained why we were there. I said we had discovered that the plaintiff was guilty of violating multiple federal criminal statutes and would be notifying the U.S. Attorney and filing a motion to dismiss the case for misconduct. I explained Cheri's discovery of the conversation and said Stu and Dick obviously didn't know we had it, that we almost certainly never would have gotten it if they had listened to the entire tape. We then played the tape, and the court reporter read aloud the false testimony Stu had just given.

Dick was blindsided, but he couldn't just sit there. He had to say something. He said one thing that was both false and foolish but another that was wise. His false statement was in response to my saying they didn't know the conversation was on the tapes they had turned over to us. Dick said he wanted the judge to know he had reviewed all the tapes before producing them. He would not have concealed anything and didn't conceal anything, and he resented any suggestion to the contrary. If that's the case, Judge Lee pointed out, Dick not only knew his client had agreed to pay a witness for his testimony, but he had also just allowed him to give false testimony about it. Dick had nothing to say in response to that. We all knew he had never heard the conversation before now.

But then Dick did something smart. Judge Lee asked our immediate plans, and I said we would return to our office and complete the deposition. I didn't add that I could hardly wait. Resuming the deposition immediately was the last thing Dick wanted, and he offered two good reasons for postponing it until the next day. The recording raised the possibility that Stu would have to invoke his fifth amendment right against self-incrimination, and the mention of Dick's purported involvement posed a potential conflict between Stu and Dick that would have to be resolved. Judge Lee said the deposition could be completed the next day.

Dick and Stu had a busy night. We learned from the court reporter that Dick called and asked her to read the crucial excerpts from Stu's testimony again. He was no doubt looking for wiggle room, but there was none. Dick and Stu then had to decide what to do, and their plan was revealed shortly after they arrived the next morning. Before I asked the first question, Stu said he needed to make a statement on the record. What he said, I had to admit, was the best they could have done.

Stu first claimed he never intended to pay Alvin a penny and never would have. Stu told Alvin he would pay him only because he knew he would never tell the truth about our client and the CFX-1 unless he thought there was something in it for him. Stu also claimed he never discussed the matter with Dick and mentioned him during the call only to make Alvin think he was serious. As for his false testimony the day before, it was a mistake, and he apologized. That was his story, and he stuck to it for the rest of the deposition.

Before we parted ways at the end of the day, Dick came up with an excuse for a return trip across Capitol Street to see Judge Lee. His purpose was to dig himself out of the hole he'd dug the day before, but he wound up just digging it deeper. He told the judge he hadn't intended to give the wrong impression the day before. The truth was that he reviewed the tapes before they were provided to us, but he obviously didn't listen to the conversation we played in chambers the day before. But the conclusion that he had listened to the conversation was exactly what he had wanted Judge Lee to believe the day before. The judge and his law clerk made eye contact. Like Judge Clark, Judge Lee was an honorable man. I'm sure he was appalled.

The trial was postponed, we filed a motion to dismiss, and the court scheduled an evidentiary hearing. Pat Barrett returned for the hearing, which lasted two days. There were four witnesses: Stu, his first lawyer, Dick, and me. It was strange to be the witness answering questions and not the lawyer asking them. I felt like I was inside a television looking out through the screen.

The highlight of the two days was getting to cross-examine Dick. Given the circumstances, he should have shown some humility, but he didn't have it in him. He apparently believed that claiming to be a big-time trial lawyer from California would sway the judge. He bragged on direct about litigating cases in many states. On cross I invited him to brag some more, and he accepted the invitation.

The best part of the cross was about a document we'd never seen before the hearing. Dick and Stu hoped to avoid dismissal by demonstrating that the CFX-1 really was defective and that everything Alvin said about it after Stu agreed to pay him for testifying was true. Dismissing the case would thus be a miscarriage of justice. The document, according to Dick, was his own handwritten notes from a purported telephone interview with Alvin that detailed all the problems with the CFX-1. Dick claimed he'd conducted the interview before our client fired Alvin, and he testified on direct that the notes of the interview would be a centerpiece of the case against our client at trial.

Interviewing Alvin while he was still employed by our client would have been a clear violation of Mississippi's ethics rules, assuming such an interview actually took place. Going through the ethical issue with Dick and watching him squirm was a pleasure, but another point occurred to me that turned into even more fun.

Because we had come so close to the trial before it was postponed, we had a signed pretrial order in place that listed all the exhibits the parties planned to offer at trial. I knew Dick's notes of the alleged interview weren't listed. We didn't have a copy of the pretrial order at the hearing because there was no reason to believe it would be relevant, but we had geography on our side. I dispatched Debra Hammack to hustle back across Capitol Street to the office and return with copies ASAP. When she handed them to me at the lectern, the questions came easy. The exchange went something like this.

"You testified earlier that your notes would be a centerpiece of your case at trial, did you not?"

"I did."

"We have a signed pretrial order in place, don't we?"

"I believe that's right." Dick was a smart guy. He probably realized what was coming, but there was nothing he could do.

"May I approach the witness, Your Honor?"

"You may."

"This is the pretrial order, isn't it?"

"It looks like it."

"This is your signature on the last page, is it not?

"It is."

"Take a look if you will at the list of exhibits the plaintiff intends to offer into evidence. These notes you've been talking about, the ones you said were going to be a centerpiece of your case at trial, they're not on the list, are they? It's a long list; take all the time you need."

Dick knew the notes weren't on the list, but again, he had to say something. To the best of my recollection, this is what he said, and it surprised me: "It's my understanding under the court's rules that a document is not required to be listed if it will be used solely for impeachment or surprise."

He was right about impeachment, though there was no witness Dick's own notes could be used to impeach. But surprise? Really? Not surprisingly, there was no surprise exception in the court's rules or, to my knowledge, in any court's rules. And how would such an exception work? What would a lawyer say? Maybe this: "This is a key document, Judge. In fact, it's the centerpiece of our case. But we didn't want the other side to know about it, so we didn't list it. We hid it, sure, but you should let us use it under the 'surprise' exception."

When Dick surprised me by invoking the non-existent "surprise" exception, I reacted with a loud one-word question: "Surprise?" Dick mumbled that maybe he was wrong about the rules.

A few days after the hearing, Judge Lee dismissed the case in a lengthy, detailed opinion. Cheri's OCD had saved our client millions. When I called Pat Barrett in the years that followed, he would answer the phone either by singing "Brooksie Baby Boy" or declaring, in his best but still terrible Southern accent, "Surprise?"

Where Everybody's Otis

Based on a complaint from a whistleblower, the Department of Justice launched a grand jury investigation of Ingalls in the 1990s for alleged mischarging. The whistleblower claimed that shipyard engineers manipulated an accounting system to shift costs from an over-budget shipbuilding contract for the Israeli government to U.S. Navy contracts.

The claim involved work performed by supervisors who were treated as Direct Apportioned Personnel (DAP) in Ingalls' accounting system. The supervisors did not charge their time directly to the contracts on which they worked. Instead, their time was automatically apportioned to the contracts on which their subordinates worked. The whistleblower alleged that supervisors gamed the system by working on the Israeli contract while their underlings worked on Navy contracts. Based on the accounting system, the time the supervisors spent on the Israeli contract was charged to the Navy.

I had never worked on a white-collar matter and was 0–1 in criminal cases for my career, having lost my case for Jerry Lynn Young after he won it without me. But Bill Powers nonetheless asked me to work with Larry Allison on the DAP grand jury investigation, which had been underway for many months before I got involved.

For two reasons, the case consumed time and resources that were grossly out of proportion to the maximum possible amount of the alleged mischarging. First, the government subpoenaed millions of documents we were certain no one ever read. But it was the government, so Ingalls had to produce them. Before I began working on the matter, twenty people were hired to process and copy the documents. Larry and I had our own offices in the building at the shipyard where the document team worked.

Second, one of the potential sanctions for mischarging was debarment. A debarment order would have prohibited Ingalls from bidding on government contracts, which would have been catastrophic not just for the company but for the economy of the entire Gulf Coast. Debarment was unlikely, but it was not a risk that could be ignored.

There were two other lawyers working on the matter when I began. Fred Stant of Virginia Beach and Bob de Luca of Philadelphia were close friends and the lawyer equivalents of Laurel and Hardy. Fred, the Stan Laurel of the duo, was tall and thin. His claim to fame was that he was the first University of Virginia basketball player to dunk in a game. Bob was neither tall nor thin. If he ever dunked a basketball, it was on an eight-foot goal. Fred was the curmudgeon, Bob the philosopher. They didn't represent Ingalls but were instead hired to serve as counsel for shipyard officials who were subpoenaed to testify before the grand jury. Larry and I couldn't represent the officials because there was a potential conflict of interest between Ingalls and them.

Working on the DAP matter led to a change in my accommodations when I went to the Coast. Larry, Fred, and Bob stayed at the Best Western Oak Manor in Biloxi, so I began staying there too. I never spent another night at the LaFont. I was riding with Fred from Biloxi to the shipyard one morning and saw blue lights on the side of the interstate ahead. When I brought them to his attention, Fred shrugged it off. "That shark's already fed," he said. "We'll just swim on by."

Oak Manor was a short walk from Mary Mahoney's, which has lines on the wall recording the high-water marks from two hurricanes—Camille in 1969 and Katrina thirty-six years later. Outside the restaurant is a magnificent live oak that once had a plaque affixed to it declaring that it was a thousand years old. The plaque may still be there; I don't know. When we asked the proprietor how he knew the tree was that old, it turned out he didn't.

The four of us became regulars in the bar and restaurant at Mary's. We even had our own waiter, an elderly gentleman named Boston, who was always jovial but would often go AWOL when we were ready for a second glass of chardonnay. Fred wanted to replace Boston with someone more attentive, but the rest of us were too attached to him. We tolerated his mediocre service and Fred's complaints about him.

The DAP matter was ultimately settled—there were no indictments, no debarment, and Ingalls paid the government a small fraction of what it spent on lawyers and the document staff—but the friendships made while we were working on it endured. Bobby Ariatti wasn't on the DAP team, but he became friends with the lawyers who were. After he took a job outside D.C. in 2011, he often drove south to visit Fred in Cape Charles, Virginia, a tiny town on the Eastern Shore across the mouth of the Chesapeake Bay from Virginia Beach.

Fred didn't live in Cape Charles, but he and a law school buddy, Tommy Stokes, bought an old duck lodge outside town half a century ago. They struggled to keep straight faces when the owner offered to sell it to them for half what they were willing to pay. Black Duck Lodge, built circa 1910, sits on a beautiful piece of property overlooking a marsh. It has six fireplaces but no air conditioning. I've never been to Fred's apartment on 57th Street in Manhattan, but I bet it's not much like the duck lodge. I bet Fred wears different clothes when he's there too. He wears worn-out, faded overalls at Black Duck.

Fred and Tommy have hosted a pig roast at the lodge every fall for many years. I've gone to Virginia three or four times to see Bobby and attend the roast. A fascinating cast of characters assembles for the gathering. One comes from the mainland by helicopter and lands in the field next to the lodge. Bob, who passed away in 2023, came several times as well, and we had reunions from our DAP days.

Until recently, Cape Charles had a business establishment that offered a rare combination: hardware and happy hour. When the weather was nice, rocking chairs would line the sidewalk outside Watson's Hardware. Owner Chip Watson, dressed in UVA orange, would hold court from his spot outside the front door. Bobby, now seventy but still youthful and vigorous, would fetch Chip's drinks from the secret stash in the back. When the weather was cold, the happy hour regulars would gather around the wood-burning stove in the middle of the store.

Cape Charles appears to be stuck in an America that no longer exists. The pace is slow, and the buildings are old. Most of the residents are old too. Because they can't stay up till midnight, the ceremonial dropping of the neon crab trap on New Year's Eve takes place at ten p.m. Cape Charles reminds me of Andy Griffith's Mayberry, but there are two key differences. Cape Charles is fact, not fiction, and it has far more than one town drunk. Many Cape Charles residents remind me of Otis.

Drinking from a Firehose

J ust after six o'clock on the morning of December 13, 1994, a massive explosion rocked the Port Neal fertilizer complex on the east bank of the Missouri River fifteen miles south of Sioux City, Iowa. Four workers were killed, another eighteen seriously injured. Effects of the blast were felt more than thirty miles away. Where a seven-story building had stood, now there was only a crater. Three thousand residents on both sides of the river were ordered to evacuate because of the risks from a cloud of ammonia. Property damage exceeded $300 million, not including losses caused by the closure of the facility for nearly a year.

The owner of the complex, Terra International, Inc., soon assembled an incident investigation committee with the stated goal of determining the cause of the explosion. After more than six months, the committee completed its work and published a report detailing its findings. Terra issued a press release and held a press conference to announce the results. The committee found the explosion occurred in a vessel called a neutralizer in which nitric acid and ammonia were combined to form ammonium nitrate. Ammonium nitrate is an effective fertilizer, but it can also be highly explosive. Just four months after the Port Neal explosion, Timothy McVeigh used it as the primary ingredient of the bomb that destroyed the Alfred P. Murrah Federal Building in Oklahoma City and killed 168.

Terra's committee was correct about the what and where of the explosion, but its conclusion about the why was far more controversial. The Environmental Protection Agency later found that the explosion was caused by Terra's faulty operations that resulted in highly acidic conditions and contaminants in the neutralizer as well as the high-temperature steam Terra used to keep the vessel's contents from freezing. The committee, by contrast, did not find that Terra's operations were at fault. Instead, the committee formed by Terra found that someone other than Terra was to blame.

The explosion, according to the committee, was caused primarily by defects in the design of the neutralizer. Specifically, the committee blamed a pipe inside the neutralizer called a sparger through which nitric acid was sprayed into the neutralizer. The sparger had multiple holes and worked like a soaker hose or spray arm of a dishwasher. The alleged problems included the material specified for the sparger, titanium, which was purportedly more combustible than available alternatives, and the hole configuration, which allowed nitric acid to pool in the bottom of the sparger when the neutralizer was not in operation. The committee concluded that the explosion initiated inside the sparger and touched off a much larger explosion outside the sparger but inside the neutralizer.

The neutralizer, it so happened, was designed by Mississippi Chemical Corporation, whose headquarters were in Yazoo City, a town of 12,500 forty-five miles northwest of Jackson. Mississippi Chemical had licensed the neutralizer design to Terra for a modest fee of $40,000. After the committee's findings were announced, the two companies lawyered-up for the litigation sure to follow. Mississippi Chemical retained Bill Smith of Brunini, and he assembled a team at the firm to work with him. Along with David Kaufman, the principal members were Patrick McDowell and Chuck McBride, who were either senior associates or new partners at the time. I was not a member of the team at the outset.

On August 31, 1995, within a five-hour span, Terra and Mississippi Chemical filed competing lawsuits, both in federal court but in different states. Each company sought home-field advantage. Terra filed in the Northern District of Iowa seeking damages for harm to the property at the Port Neal complex and business interruption. Mississippi Chemical filed in the Southern District of Mississippi and requested a declaratory judgment that the neutralizer design was blameless as well as actual and punitive damages for defamation.

Early efforts focused on where the dispute would be litigated. Primarily because of a forum-selection clause in the license agreement requiring disputes to be decided in Mississippi, Mississippi Chemical prevailed. The Mississippi court denied Terra's transfer motion, the Iowa court granted Mississippi Chemical's similar motion, and the Eighth Circuit affirmed its conclusion. The dispute would be litigated in Mississippi.

The case was assigned to Judge Bramlette and would be tried in Natchez. Years later, not long before the scheduled trial date, a reporter for the *Natchez Democrat* wrote an article about the benefits to the city's economy the proceeding was likely to have. The notion that the lawyers would go shopping when trial wasn't in session struck me as doubtful, though we would have to eat.

After the venue issue was decided, the parties exchanged discovery requests, produced many thousands of documents, and began taking depositions. They also hired large teams of experts, including specialists in explosions, kinetics, metallurgy, and accounting. A key issue was whether the sparger exploded internally or was destroyed by an external explosion. Analyzing the sparger fragments was crucial. Because the sparger was the only piece of equipment in the entire facility that was made of titanium, identifying even small fragments was possible. Some were found on the bottom of a pond far from the site of the neutralizer.

After more than two years of constant activity, there was a change of personnel on the team representing Mississippi Chemical. In late 1997, the company hired Bill Smith away from the Brunini firm. He went from being lead outside counsel in a bet-the-company case to lead in-house counsel. In his new role as general counsel, he would be responsible for overseeing all the company's legal work, including the Terra litigation.

After Bill started his new job, one of his first acts was to ask me to join the team of Brunini lawyers representing the company on the Terra case. There was already an excellent team in place, but Bill recognized that another experienced litigator would be needed. After making sure I had the time available that would be necessary to work on the case, I began the task of learning everything the rest of the team had spent more than two years learning. For the next few months, I drank from a firehose.

While the firehose was still gushing, I entered the fray. We had a great team—good friends working hard together—and it was a great case. There were excellent lawyers on both sides. Randy Duncan and Steve Eckley were our Iowa co-counsel. Terra had a fine group of lawyers from Mayer, Brown & Platt in Chicago led by Rick McCombs and Javier Rubinstein. Natie Caraway and my friend George Ritter were their Mississippi co-counsel.

The lawyers were all professional and collegial. We resolved most disputes without the need for court intervention, disagreed without being disagreeable, and litigated as efficiently as possible. I spent many days deposing Terra's experts at a large, square table in a conference room in Mayer Brown's offices. In the middle of the table was a hole for telephone lines and such. On several occasions, we settled scheduling issues by pitching pennies. The Mayer Brown lawyers called us the Brunini Boys and, we learned years later, the Four Horsemen of the Apocalypse. It was all very civilized and respectful.

We also had the benefit of an excellent trial judge. Judge Bramlette was the kind of Southerner who is underestimated at their peril by those from outside the South. He graduated from Princeton, then became an accomplished lawyer and an excellent judge, but he was Southern to the core in speech, manner, and conduct. He lived on a farm outside Woodville, a tiny town in the southwest corner of Mississippi, and spent his spare time hunting and fishing. The case was set for trial in Natchez because it was forty miles from Woodville, which was not as close to anywhere else with a federal courthouse.

On one occasion, after the parties had filed a flurry of motions,

Judge Bramlette scheduled a status conference and oral arguments in Jackson. We began the day by meeting in chambers he had borrowed from one of the Jackson judges. The four Brunini Boys took seats on one side of a long conference table, and seven lawyers representing Terra—five from Mayer Brown plus Natie and George—were on the other. Judge Bramlette joined us, said good morning, and took the seat at the end of the table. Then he said this: "Gentlemen, we've got a lot to deal with here. I've been catching 'em faster than I can string 'em."

The lawyers from Chicago looked perplexed. If they knew what the judge was catching and stringing, it didn't show. I figured one of them would ask Natie or George at a break, and it would go something like this:

"What was that he said at the beginning? Catching them faster than he could what?"

"String 'em. Fish. He was talking about fish."

"What's fish got to do with anything?"

"Nothing really. The fish are the motions we've been filing. And we've been filing 'em faster that he can read 'em."

"Sometimes I don't understand you guys down here."

"Y'all. 'You guys' down here are y'all."

The Pirate and the Parrot

Two of my favorite members of our team were neither lawyers nor witnesses. At least that was the plan at the beginning. Abid Kemal was a young immigrant from Pakistan who lived and worked on the West Coast. He had long dark hair and the look of a Barbary pirate. He was single and handsome and turned the heads of women when we walked by. If a movie had been made about the lawsuit, Johnny Depp would have played him. Jimmie Carol Oxley appeared on the surface to be Abid's polar opposite. She was white, middle-aged, and married, lived three thousand miles from Abid, and looked nothing like Johnny Depp.

But beneath the surface, the two had much in common. Both were brilliant scientists, experts in explosions who were passionate about their work, and delightful dinner companions. And we hired both for the same purpose. Abid and Jimmie were retained as consulting experts to help the lawyers on our team understand the complex scientific questions at the heart of the case and assist our testifying experts with their work.

I was responsible for deposing Kim Clark, an accomplished scientist and Terra's principal expert on the cause of the explosion. The deposition was a lengthy undertaking. I would question Dr. Clark for a day or two, he would do more work and conduct more tests, then I would fly back to Chicago and question him some more. In one of our sessions, the court reporter interrupted and said I was talking too fast. I said I wanted the record to reflect that the court reporter from Chicago told the lawyer from Mississippi to slow down. I wound up deposing Dr. Clark for a total of seven days. It was a lifetime record for me and probably one for him. My attention span was longer then.

Abid and Jimmie provided the expertise I needed to depose an expert with Dr. Clark's credentials. They helped me prepare, attended most sessions of the deposition, and gave me suggestions during breaks. After I turned in at night, they would stay up late discussing the issues. I was awakened in the wee hours on more than one occasion by a rustling sound. It was Abid and Jimmie sliding sheets of paper covered with their handwritten notes under the door of my hotel room. I would rise early to study them.

During one of my sessions with Dr. Clark, I checked the morning paper and saw the Cubs were in the middle of a homestand. It must have been in the summer of 1999. When I saw they had an afternoon game starting at 3:30, I told Terra's lawyers I wanted to stop for the day at 2:30 so I could take Abid to see the Cubs at Wrigley Field. Jimmie wasn't there, perhaps for the reason I'll get to shortly. The lawyers said sure. It was all very civilized.

Abid was a devoted fan of cricket and knew everything there was to know about it, but he knew nothing at all about baseball. I mean nothing. I spent our lunch break trying to explain the game to him. Abid was a quick study, but we didn't have much time. I covered the basics but didn't get to the balk or infield fly rule, or the fact that it's a strikeout if you foul off a bunt with two strikes. Baseball is not a simple game.

I had been to Wrigley only once and was excited that my second trip would be not only Abid's first but his first time ever to see a baseball game. Wrigley Field is a shrine. With its ivy-covered outfield walls, it's one of the most famous and beautiful stadiums in all the world. A trip to Wrigley is a Bucket List item for baseball fans. For a man to see his very first game there would be like ringing the doorbell for his very first date and having Salma Hayek greet him.

I thought my plans were well-laid, but after lunch they went awry. First, Abid realized he might miss his flight home if he went to the game and decided he would have to pass. My noon tutorial had been a waste. But no matter. I had my heart set on the outing to Wrigley and wasn't going to let Abid's loss be my loss. As planned, I would stop the deposition at 2:30 and take me out to the ball game.

But even that plan went awry. When I asked one of my last questions of the day, George Zelcs, the lawyer for Terra's insurers, interrupted before the witness could answer. I looked over at George. He wasn't looking at me or the witness but was instead looking down at his laptop. He was smiling. He hadn't objected to my question, and it took me a second for the significance of his words to sink in.

What George had said was "strike one." Strike one? How could that be? The game didn't start for an hour. Then it dawned on me. The game time I'd seen in *USA Today* must have been in eastern time, not central. Like my buddies who called me at three in the morning in my first semester at Duke, I didn't take account of the difference. The Cubs' pitcher had thrown a strike on the first pitch of the game, and George had announced the umpire's call. I finished quickly, rushed to the train, and made it to my seat in the right field stands as fast as I could. The fifth inning was ending. I watched the last four. I don't recall who won the game, but I remember the first pitch.

Though Jimmie was in her mid-forties, she became pregnant during the course of the lawsuit and gave birth while it was going full steam. Perhaps that's why she wasn't in Chicago for the Wrigley Field fiasco, when Abid missed the whole game and I missed most of it.

Shortly after Jimmie's baby was born, we had a team meeting in Jackson. With a newborn to care for, Jimmie couldn't travel, so she called in and participated by speaker phone. We would forget she was on the line, but every now and then a terrible sound would come blasting through the speaker. I had three children by then and was familiar with the sound normal babies make. This sounded nothing like that. It was more screech than cry.

When we heard the noise, worried looks were exchanged in the conference room. I suspect we were all asking ourselves the same questions: What is wrong with that poor child? Isn't it risky for a woman Jimmie's age to have a baby? We may have been asking ourselves, but we couldn't very well ask Jimmie.

But it turned out there was no reason to worry. At some point we decided Jimmie needed to take on a bigger role in the case and designated her to testify as an expert. Her deposition was scheduled, and Chuck McBride flew to Rhode Island to help her get ready. One of our summer clerks, Johnny Brunini, who would soon become the fourth generation of his family to practice in the firm, went with him.

Chuck had arranged to meet with Jimmie at her home on the Atlantic Seaboard, where she taught chemistry at the University of Rhode Island. Chuck and Johnny admired the view of the ocean from her kitchen window, then turned their attention to Jimmie. She sat at the kitchen table, ready to get to work. Her workpapers were spread out before her. The baby slept. A parrot sat on its perch nearby.

They got to work, but before long Chuck and Johnny heard a cry. It was the baby. To their relief, the baby sounded like a baby. A woman brought the infant to Jimmie to be nursed. Jimmie handled the task discreetly, but she didn't fool the bird. Wanting a bird's-eye view, the parrot left its perch, glided across the room, and landed on Jimmie's shoulder. Once there, the pecking began. As the baby nursed, the jealous bird hopped back and forth from Jimmie's left shoulder to her right, then back to her left, pecking her arms all the time. Chuck put two and two together. The parrot, the source of the terrible sounds we'd heard over the speaker phone, must have been an only child before the newborn came along. It was interspecies jealousy.

I wasn't there, but if I close my eyes, I can picture it. A new mother, a nursing infant, a jealous parrot, waves crashing on the shore. If only Abid had been there, complete with eyepatch and peg leg, the tableau would have been complete. The scene wasn't what Chuck had envisioned when he invited a summer clerk to accompany him, but it was better than shooting him.

Wasted Nights

Papers pushed under the door of my room in the middle of the night were not the only cause of sleepless nights during my work for Mississippi Chemical. Flight delays were another. In the summer of 1999, during thunderstorm season, I managed to accumulate three complimentary Delta Air Lines toiletry kits in the span of six weeks.

I remember two sleepless nights well, one caused by a flight delay and the other by clotheslessness. On the first occasion, I was scheduled to be in Tulsa the next day to depose an engineer who was a member of Terra's incident investigation committee. My flight left Jackson in late afternoon. Even with a layover in Dallas, I would arrive in Tulsa in plenty of time to get a good night's sleep.

But once again, my best-laid plans went awry. A storm front was moving east across Texas. My flight was heading straight toward it. The pilot detoured south. We circled, then landed somewhere. I don't remember where, but it wasn't Dallas. The storm system stalled, and we sat and waited. A break finally came, and we took off for the second time. We landed in Dallas at eleven. By then, my flight to Tulsa was long gone. I booked the earliest flight the next morning, then began efforts to find a room.

I struck out. American had cancelled every outbound flight, and a gate attendant told me no rooms were available in the Dallas metropolitan area. Maybe that was hyperbole, but I gave up. Delta put out blankets, coffee, and Biscoff cookies, and I set out to find a quiet place to try to get some sleep. I spotted a dark and empty gate and decided to make it my quarters for the night. My briefcase would serve as my pillow. It was all I had.

Sleeping on a hard surface would be a challenge, but I was used to sleeping on the ground when I went camping. I figured I could do it. But there was a factor I hadn't counted on that made sleeping in DFW much harder than sleeping in the woods. I walked into the gate and *BAM*, the lights came on. They were on a motion detector, and I was moving. Were all the gates like this? Surely not, I thought. I walked down the concourse and tried another one. *BAM*. I tried a third. *BAM*. I gave up, lay down under the lights, and put one arm over my eyes. Hard floor, bright lights, big city. This was worse than the La Font.

After a few minutes, the bright lights went off. Blessed relief. But the relief didn't last. Just as I was about to doze off, I rolled over in search of a more comfortable position. *BAM* again. I covered my eyes again and waited. The lights went off again. I began to doze off again but didn't quite make it. This time it was my ear. It itched. I scratched. *BAM* for the third time in this gate, the fifth altogether.

"And all the news just repeats itself, like some forgotten dream that we've both seen." Those lines are from "Hello in There," John Prine's beautiful ballad about an older couple who lost a son in the Korean War and still don't know what for. As I lay alone on the floor of a gate in DFW, it wasn't the news that repeated itself. It was darkness, motion, *BAM*, darkness, motion, *BAM*. I wanted desperately to sleep. I felt as old and sad as the couple in the song.

I rose at dawn, stiff and sore, and caught my flight to Tulsa. I spent the entire day deposing the engineer about the technical aspects of the explosion and his work on the committee. It was a tough slog, but I was much younger then. When I read the transcript weeks later, I was pleased to see that I was semi-coherent at least some of the time.

My second sleepless night came much later. I was alone again, but this time I was at the Four Seasons in Chicago. And this time it was my own fault, not that of a missed flight or lights on motion sensors.

I had flown to Chicago three days earlier. My plan was to take a short follow-up deposition the next morning, then fly home. I packed light, with an extra shirt and boxers, but no extra pants. I could wear the same pair two days in a row. No problem. But, yet again, my plans went awry.

One of Terra's lawyers came into the conference room during the deposition and asked to confer with me. Bill Smith and David Kaufman were flying up to Chicago for a meeting the next day to discuss settlement. I was to extend my reservation and stay another night.

My light packing was now a problem. I bought a pair of boxers at a department store on Michigan Avenue so I would at least have fresh underwear for the next day, fresh lettuce as a college buddy called it. I wore one of my shirts again and my only pair of pants for the third day in a row. We reached a deal on the key terms by late afternoon and agreed to iron out the details the following morning.

The Terra lawyers took us to dinner that night at an Italian place. I don't remember the name of the restaurant, which I believe was on the South Side, but I remember two things about it. The food was fabulous, and Rick McCombs told us the man who painted all the artwork was more than just an artist. He was also a mob hit man and was currently serving a life sentence in the big house.

When I returned to my room, I considered the possibility that my light packing might now be a problem not just for me but for everyone who would be near me. I had no fresh lettuce, my pants could almost stand up on their own, and I would have to wear "my cleanest dirty shirt," to quote Kris Kristofferson.

I decided to take advantage of the Four Seasons dry-cleaning service. Put your clothes in a bag, hang them outside your door, and they reappear before dawn, clean and pressed. Easy peasy. Before I turned in, I bagged up every stitch of clothes I had and hung them on the exterior doorknob.

I woke with a start at one in the morning. What if? What if they didn't bring my clothes back in time? What if they hadn't even taken them? This was the Four Seasons, but still. I walked to the door and cracked it open. The bag was gone. Step one in the process had been accomplished. It was a good sign, but instead of relief I began to worry about step two. If the clothes didn't make it back in time, I'd be in a real pickle. I was down to the outfit I was born in and would be stuck in the room. I tossed and turned.

But as in the case of Jimmie and her baby, there was no need for concern. I heard a noise outside my door at five o'clock, waited a minute or two so I wouldn't flash the noisemaker, then cracked open the door again. There were my clothes, clean and pressed. I wore the same pair of pants for the fourth day in a row, but now they had a fresh crease. We finalized the agreement, then I flew home to Jackson.

Apples and Water Buffaloes

I ssues involving metallurgy were crucial to the case. We had three experts on the subject matter, all hired before I joined the team. Two were Ed Shanley of MIT and Charlie Rau, who lived in Arizona and worked for an extraordinary company called Exponent Failure Analysis, which also employed Abid and others who assisted on the case. The name of the third expert escapes me. If it comes to me, the preceding sentence won't be in the book. All three were very helpful, and Charlie proved to be essential to our successful resolution of the case.

The experts focused on two of Terra's central claims: (1) that the neutralizer design was defective because it specified that the sparger was to be made of titanium and (2) that the fragments established that the explosion initiated inside the sparger. Our experts categorically rejected both claims.

Not long after I joined the team, several of us flew to Boston to meet with Dr. Shanley. He was in his eighties but still fit and trim and an active snow skier. He scoffed at Terra's claim that titanium was a poor choice for the sparger. To the best of my recollection, someone on Terra's team, perhaps the incident investigation committee, had compared the combustibility of metals in powder form and determined that titanium was more combustible than available alternatives. The notion that metals could be combustible at all seemed odd to me, but Dr. Shanley said most metals are combustible in powder form. Many, he told us, will ignite merely from the friction of going through the air if ground finely enough and thrown hard enough. At least that's the way I recall it from a quarter of a century ago.

But this much I remember clearly. He said it was absurd to

compare the flammability of metal powder to that of a solid pipe and that a titanium pipe was no more combustible than one made of stainless steel. In fact, neither was combustible at all. The issue was one of surface to volume. Just as it's much easier to light a twig than a log, metal powder is far more flammable than a metal pipe.

When I understood the issue, I coined an expression that I still use. I said this wasn't like comparing apples and oranges, which are both small and round and fruit. This was like comparing apples and water buffaloes.

Not a Bad Day

O ur metallurgy experts, especially Charlie Rau, viewed the analysis of the sparger fragments by Terra's expert with disdain. Charlie believed the evidence for an explosion outside the sparger was unmistakable and used unkind words to describe the claim that the fragments supported the opposite conclusion. No legitimate scientist could possibly believe that, he said. Charlie's certainty led to the strategy that in turn led to the settlement of the case.

Federal Rule of Evidence 706 authorizes a judge to appoint his own expert. I saw it happen only once in my career, and this was it. Because Charlie was so confident, we decided to file a motion asking Judge Bramlette to appoint his own expert to analyze the sparger fragments. The other Brunini Boys credit me with the idea. I don't recall one way or the other, but because of the way it turned out, who am I to quibble?

We got the okay from Mississippi Chemical, filed the motion, and explained the procedure we envisioned. The parties would nominate qualified candidates to serve in the role, and the judge would choose one. The fragments would then be boxed up and shipped to the chosen expert, who would decide if the explosion initiated inside or outside the sparger based on his analysis of the fragments and written submissions from the parties.

Our motion came out of nowhere and must have been a shock to Terra's team. As the deadline for their response neared, we speculated about what they would do. When the time came, they opposed it. There could have been valid reasons—the lawyers may have liked where they stood in the case, and a court-appointed expert would be a wild card—but their opposition made them look bad. The trial judge now knew that Mississippi Chemical

was willing to have a neutral expert examine the fragments, but Terra was not.

Judge Bramlette scheduled a hearing on the motion in Jackson. David argued it, and the judge granted it on the spot. David recalled that I poked him in the back when it became clear the ruling was going our way. The parties nominated candidates, Judge Bramlette picked one, and the fragments were shipped to him in California.

And that's where things stood when settlement talks began in earnest and I got stuck in Chicago with one pair of pants. We all realized the expert's decision would be crucial. It would be very hard for either side to question the conclusion of an accomplished expert who was not being paid by the other. If he found the explosion initiated outside the sparger, Terra was almost certain to lose. Their defective-design case depended entirely on an internal explosion. On the other hand, if he found there was an internal explosion, we could still point to Terra's poor operating practices, but it would be hard to deny that the sparger design played a role.

This is where Charlie became crucial to settling the case. I was asked by clients many times to assess the likelihood of a favorable result and often said we should win or the odds were in our favor, but I never told a client we couldn't possibly lose. But that's essentially what Charlie told Mississippi Chemical and its liability insurers, who would play a key role in funding any settlement. When they asked him to predict the court-appointed expert's decision, Charlie had the courage of his convictions. He told them there was an 85% chance the expert would find the explosion initiated outside the sparger, a 15% chance he would be unable to reach a conclusion, and no chance at all that he would find the explosion initiated inside the sparger.

Charlie's confidence made the settlement possible. The insurers were persuaded to offer a generous amount if the expert ruled against us because Charlie convinced them he wouldn't rule against us. The expert's finding, as yet unknown, was central to the proposal we made and to the agreement the parties reached. The key terms of the deal were these: If the expert found in Terra's favor, Mississippi Chemical's insurers would pay Terra the remaining policy limits, approximately $90 million, and Mississippi Chemical's defamation claim would be dismissed. If he found in our favor, Mississippi Chemical would be awarded a judgment of $18 million on its defamation claim, and Terra's claims would be dismissed.

The ratio of five to one may seem high, but Terra was claiming more than half a billion dollars in actual damages and, try as we might, we couldn't find that Mississippi Chemical had suffered any financial harm from being blamed by Terra's committee for the explosion. There was one more material provision of the settlement. If Judge Bramlette's expert could not reach a conclusion, the settlement would be off, and we would resume trial preparation. We finalized the deal in June 2000 and waited for the expert to complete his analysis and report his findings.

And while we waited, we quit working and rested. It was about time. The lawyers on both sides had been going non-stop for many months. Based on the Brunini firm's expectation that each lawyer would bill 1900 hours a year, I had worked the equivalent of nine and a half months in the first six months of 2000. I'm sure David, Patrick, and Chuck had worked just as much. I took my ten-year-old son Paul to Colorado for two weeks in July and scheduled another two-week vacation in August, half lounging at the beach with my family, half hiking in the mountains with Bobby Ariatti.

One day while we were at the beach, I called my secretary Cherie Arthur to check in and see if there was any news on the Terra case. She said none, then told me to hold on a minute. Yelling was coming from the direction of David's office at the end of the hall. She transferred me to him, and he explained the yelling. Judge Bramlette had scheduled a conference call with the lawyers on both sides to read them the expert's report. He had found the explosion initiated outside the sparger. Charlie had been right all along. A lawsuit that could have resulted in bankruptcy for Mississippi Chemical ended in a judgment for $18 million in its favor. It was not a bad day, not a bad day at all.

Three days after we learned the news, I drove west from the beach to New Orleans and flew west to Spokane, where Bobby picked me up at the airport and we drove west some more. That night, I am confident, I became the first man in the history of men to camp beside Grand Coulee Dam in Washington after spending the night before in Seagrove Beach, Florida. We rose the next morning and spent the next five days backpacking in the Cascades. It was a magnificent trip, except for the black flies, but that was a story for a different book.

The lawsuit was over, but there were related matters to conclude. David took charge while I went on vacations. But months later, I was drafted to play a minor role in one remaining matter.

Mississippi Chemical had asserted a claim against the firm that employed one of the members of Terra's incident investigation committee based on alleged misconduct in his work on the committee. Another settlement meeting in Chicago, this time involving a different dispute, was scheduled. David would attend with Bill Smith, and Randy Duncan would fly over from Des Moines. Shortly before takeoff, Bill decided I needed to go with them. I had deposed the committee member and knew more about his testimony and his role on the committee than anyone else on our team.

I tried to beg off, but Bill was insistent. He was the client, so I called Betsy Ann and asked her to pack me a hanging bag and meet us at the airport. I would have extra pants this time. As I was walking out the door, I asked Cherie to book me a room at the Drake, the wonderful hotel on Michigan Avenue that is now more than a century old. That's where the others were staying, but as we pulled up at the airport, Cherie called with bad news. The Drake was full. I began ticking off a list of the other places in Chicago where I'd stayed during the lawsuit. Cherie, who was an outstanding secretary, had already checked them all. They were all full. I again tried to beg off. Bill again insisted. He was still the client, so I still went. Before we took off, I called Cherie back and asked her to keep trying.

As soon as we landed, I called Cherie again and was greeted with even worse news. There was a huge medical convention in the city, and there were no rooms available within twenty-five miles of downtown. I was reminded of my night in DFW. But at least I wouldn't have to sleep in the airport. Cherie had reserved a room for me in a suburb thirty minutes away. I rode in the cab to the Drake with Bill and David, hoping something would work out.

Randy was waiting for us in the lobby, and the three of them lined up to check in. I lined up behind them, but I don't know why. I didn't have a reservation, and the hotel was full. All the hotels were full. What would I say when I got to the front of the line? I felt like Snoopy waiting in line at the movie behind Charlie Brown and Lucy.

After the others had checked in and it was my turn, the clerk didn't ask if I had a reservation. I would have told the truth, but that wasn't his question. He just asked for my name and, like my star witness, I said only what was necessary to answer him. He looked down, started typing, and a pained expression came over his face. He had seen from looking up that I was with the others, and he saw from looking down that I had no reservation. He also may have seen that I'd stayed at the Drake lots of times.

I remained silent, hoping for the best. He typed some more, then smiled. "Mr. Eason," he said, "We seem to have misplaced your reservation. We have no regular rooms available. If it's alright with you, we'll put you in the Michigan Suite. It's a penthouse on the top floor. I believe you'll find it quite satisfactory. And you will of course be charged only the regular room rate. Will that be acceptable?" I said it would.

The four of us had a wonderful dinner at Spiaggi, a fine Italian restaurant on the corner of Michigan Avenue and Oak Street. Wine flowed, and truffles were shaved. We then repaired to my penthouse to have an after-dinner drink, reminisce about the case, and gaze out over moonlit Lake Michigan. The firm that employed the committee member agreed to settle the claim the next day. It was a fitting conclusion to a great case.

Oozing Down the Table

Not long after the Mississippi Chemical case ended, I was presented with a rare opportunity, at least for me. I was asked to handle a case for a plaintiff on a contingency fee. My client would be David Woods, owner of a defunct Volvo truck dealership south of Jackson. The defendant would be Volvo Trucks of North America. David claimed Volvo had promised to provide him with financial assistance when his dealership was in dire straits. But when the time came to put its money where its mouth was, Volvo reneged, and the dealership went under.

I took an immediate liking to David and wanted to represent him. After I kicked the tires and interviewed his accountant, I secured the firm's blessing and agreed to take the case. Our suit was filed in federal court in Jackson and assigned to Judge Wingate.

Dan Goldstein, an excellent trial lawyer from Baltimore, was lead counsel for Volvo. He and I swapped our accustomed roles for the case. I worked in a big firm, at least by Jackson standards, and normally defended corporations. Now my client was not only a plaintiff but a real live human being. Dan was a partner in a small firm and represented plaintiffs in civil rights cases and criminal defendants. Now his client was the big company accused of mistreating the little guy.

Taking a case on a contingency was also a new experience for me. It gave me a new respect for plaintiffs' lawyers who handle nearly all their cases on contingencies. The prospect of losing any case is stressful enough, but not getting paid if you lose makes the stress far worse. At least it did for me.

I had to prove two key facts to win the case: that Volvo promised David financial assistance and that the assistance would have been enough to save his dealership. There were no smoking-gun documents on the first issue, which came down to a he said/he said credibility dispute. But I had one distinct advantage: My he, David, was infinitely more likable and believable than Volvo's he, a dealer development manager I'll call Dick. David claimed Dick was the one who had promised him the assistance.

Some lawyers ask a litany of process questions at the beginning of depositions before getting to any substance. Common ones include: "Is there any reason you can't give a deposition today?" "Do you understand that I'll be asking you questions?" "And that you are required to answer them?" "You realize you're under oath, don't you?" Questions like that.

I never had the patience for such questions and concluded they were a waste of time early in my career. I typically asked one process question, some variation of this: "If I ask you a question that's not clear or you don't understand, don't answer it. Just tell me, and I'll ask a better question. Is that fair?" I started with this because I didn't want a witness to claim later he didn't understand a question. And of the many hundreds of witnesses I deposed, all of them, with but one exception, agreed that my request was fair.

Dick was the one exception. David and I flew to Greensboro, North Carolina, home of Volvo's corporate offices, for me to depose the company's witnesses. We hired a videographer to record Dick's deposition so we could present it to the jury at trial. I started the deposition with my standard process question and was met with a surprising response. Dick said something like this: "I don't know if that's fair or not. I might not realize I don't understand a question. I might not realize a question is not clear. So no, I can't agree to that." Dan, seated beside Dick, sighed.

Dick got worse from there. He was squirrelly and evasive; he dodged and weaved. He even had a seedy little mustache. I couldn't stand the guy, which was always a good sign. At the first break, after Dan and Dick had left David and me in the conference room with the court reporter and videographer, I announced my verdict: "What a slimeball."

The videographer chimed in. "Yeah, and it's oozing down the table."

That was another good sign. If the case came down to David

versus Dick, I felt good about our chances. But whether the financial assistance would have saved the dealership depended on more than David's credibility. We had dueling experts on the issue, David's accountant and one hired by Volvo for the case.

Our accountant was far better than Volvo's. When I deposed theirs, it became obvious he was not qualified to offer the opinions Volvo wanted him to give and couldn't provide any basis in the evidence for them. I was surprised an accomplished lawyer like Dan had chosen the guy and asked Dan where he found him. Dan said he was recommended by his local counsel, whose discernment about witnesses did not live up to his sterling credentials.

But there were potential flaws in our expert's opinions too. Dan and I filed dueling motions, so-called Daubert motions, to exclude the dueling experts. After a wait of many months, Judge Wingate scheduled a hearing on the two motions. Excluding Volvo's expert was an easy call—Dan didn't put up much of a fight—but our expert was a much closer case. In the end, a math mistake did him in. Dan walked him through his calculations on cross-examination and exposed the error, which he'd relied on in reaching his conclusions. Judge Wingate declared a pox on both of our experts and barred them both from testifying at trial.

I was sick about the outcome. Both parties had lost their experts, but my client had the burden of proof. Without an accountant to attest that the financial assistance would have saved the dealership, I was afraid Judge Wingate would throw our case out before we made it to the jury. David would go home empty-handed, and there would be no fee for all the work I'd done. I decided contingency fees were not for me. I still had a wife and three kids, one of whom was now in college, and I didn't want my income to depend on the accuracy of someone else's calculations.

Not long after the hearing, we began settlement talks. Volvo was willing to pay much more than I expected, and we wound up reaching an agreement in the high six figures. Most of the money went to David's creditors, our fee was less than I'd hoped when I took the case, but we came out far better than I had feared after Judge Wingate excluded our expert.

When the dust settled, I told Dan I was surprised Volvo had paid so much. He was gracious and said they feared I would come up with some way to overcome the loss of our expert. That may have been part of it, but I suspect the slime oozing down the table in Greensboro was a bigger factor.

The Robuss Colonel

In the early 2000s, I gave myself two nicknames. I came up with one of them myself. The other one was a gift from a plaintiff.

A young man I'll call Tommy clerked at the Brunini firm after his first year of law school in the summer of 2002. He was a fine young man and an excellent student, and he's now a fine lawyer. But he had other qualities that led to my nickname. One was that he was well raised by Southern parents who taught him to respect his elders, the other that he was a tad naïve and gullible. Maybe more than a tad.

Being taught to respect his elders is the trait that got the ball rolling. When Tommy showed up for the summer, I was in my mid-forties, exactly twice his age, and he refused to call me Brooks. I was Mr. Eason to Tommy, and that's what he called me. I told him to stop. Mr. Eason was my father, I said. I was Tommy's elder, so I got to call the shots.

But Tommy didn't obey. He kept calling me Mr. Eason, and I kept telling him to knock it off. He cited his upbringing as an excuse. He wasn't comfortable calling me Brooks, and he couldn't bring himself to do it. I threatened him. I said I would fire him if he didn't stop. He knew I was bluffing, and I remained Mr. Eason to him.

When he called me Mr. Eason for the umpteenth time, I had an epiphany. "Just call me Colonel," I said. He saluted. Problem solved. For the next few weeks, we had what I thought was an inside joke. He would see me coming down the hall, snap to attention, and say, "Morning, Colonel." I would say "at ease" as I walked past. He didn't call me Brooks, but he didn't call me Mr. Eason either. We were both satisfied with the compromise.

After work one day, a group of lawyers and summer clerks went out for drinks. One of the clerks asked me if I'd gone straight through school before joining the firm. I responded with a quick history—high school in Tupelo, undergrad at Ole Miss, law school at Duke, a year with Judge Clark, Brunini ever since.

Tommy looked confused and asked a question of his own. "But when were you in the military?"

It took me a minute, but then I realized what he meant. "You mean you believed me?" I asked.

"Sure," Tommy answered. "I told my father I was working for a colonel."

"Tell him you're not."

Many years ago, a fine young man named Jonny Drake lived with Betsy Ann and our children and me during his senior year of high school before attending West Point and joining the Army. Many years later, after serving combat tours in Iraq and Afghanistan and becoming a full-bird colonel, Jonny came to see us with his wife and four children. When I told Jonny and his teenage son Daniel about my impersonation of a colonel two decades before, Daniel responded with a straight face and two words: "stolen valor."

"Well played," I said.

I was reminded of my brief stint as a colonel and added this story to the book when I ran into Tommy in downtown Jackson in early 2024. He was now exactly the same age I was when he called me Mr. Eason and then Colonel. This time he called me Brooks.

The second nickname I gave myself came from a plaintiff in an Ingalls employment case. I don't remember the plaintiff's name or what his lawsuit was about, but I recall his appearance and something he said.

He was yet another welder, but he looked even less the part than Dawn in her yellow bikini. He was a tiny man—I'm guessing 5'4" and 125—and a natty dresser. When he appeared for me to take his deposition, he looked to be dressed for an evening of ballroom dancing. He wore a freshly starched shirt, perfectly creased pants, and a handsome sport coat, his outfit topped off by a tweed Ascot cap. The welder answering the questions was far more dapper than the lawyer asking them.

The sharp-dressed man complained in his deposition that the other members of his welding crew picked on him. They called him a sissy, he claimed. He denied the charge. "I'm not a sissy," he declared. "I'm a robuss man."

I had not heard the t at the end of robust, and I wanted to make sure I heard him right. "You're a what?" I asked.

"I'm a robuss man," he said. "I'm not a sissy."

After the deposition, I decided I would be a robuss man too. I'm not as robuss as I used to be, but I still claim the title. And when I do something that requires superhuman strength—for example, when I open a jar Carrie can't open—I remind her that she's married to a robuss man.

Right Accent at the Right Time

Two agricultural companies located six hundred miles apart on the Mississippi River began a serious courtship in the mid-1990s. One was much larger than the other. Monsanto, one of the leading biotech companies in the world, was headquartered just west of the river in St. Louis. Delta and Pineland Company, a cottonseed company, could be found at One Cotton Row in Scott, Mississippi, a tiny company town less than five miles east of the river.

Though the companies were very different, each had something of value to offer the other. Monsanto had developed transgenic traits that could be inserted into cottonseed to make crops healthier and more profitable. There were two principal traits. One was Bollgard, which gave cotton plants resistance to that scourge of cotton farmers, the detestable boll weevil. The other was Round-Up Ready, a Monsanto product that protected cotton plants from another Monsanto product. Farmers could spray their Round-Up Ready cotton fields with Round-Up, and the weeds would die, the cotton would thrive, and yields would surge.

In the meantime, the small but growing company in Scott was implementing an ambitious plan to expand its distribution business internationally. Delta Pine formed joint ventures in Singapore and China and expanded its market share in Mexico, Greece, and Spain. By 1994, the company was selling cottonseed in thirteen countries, many in South America.

Monsanto had the traits, Delta Pine the seeds and sales force. It was a match made in heaven. There was synergy, and the relationship blossomed. They entered into a collaborative research agreement in late 1995, then a series of international joint ventures. They held hands, kissed, and engaged in corporate foreplay.

Monsanto popped the question in early 1998, and Delta Pine said yes. Monsanto would acquire Delta Pine in a stock-for-stock transaction. The smaller company would cease to exist, Delta Pine's shareholders would become Monsanto shareholders, and all the shareholders, both old and new, would have a Merry Christmas.

But as happens so often, one of the parties to the engagement got cold feet. At least that's what the other one claimed. Per Delta Pine, once the ring was on its finger, Monsanto developed buyer's remorse. The bloom was off the cotton plant. The merger agreement required Monsanto to use its best efforts to obtain antitrust approval from the Department of Justice, but Delta Pine claimed its merger partner just went through the motions. Monsanto wouldn't even come to Mississippi to help pick out the china.

Delta Pine, having pledged itself to Monsanto, was left at home on weekends, lonely and alone, eating Ben & Jerry's and watching reruns of *Lawrence Welk*. No other suitors came calling. And while Monsanto's stock price soared, Delta Pine's plummeted. From Monsanto's perspective far upriver, the price of the dowry was now much too high. At the end of 1999, having failed to obtain DOJ approval for the transaction, Monsanto called it off.

Like Terra and Mississippi Chemical four years before, the two companies soon lawyered-up and filed competing lawsuits. Because both were organized under Delaware law, there was no jurisdiction in federal court. The dispute would have to be litigated in state court. Which state was the question. Delta Pine, like Mississippi Chemical before it, wanted home-court advantage. The company sued Monsanto for breach of contract in the Circuit Court of the First Judicial District of Bolivar County, Mississippi, the county where Scott is located. The courthouse was in Rosedale, a river town far past its prime. Monsanto, wanting no part of a Mississippi forum, reacted by filing suit in Chancery Court in Delaware.

Not long after the suits were filed, the presiding judges in the two cases conducted hearings. Delta Pine's lead counsel, Allen Kezsbom of New York's Fried Frank, presented a compelling argument to the judge in Delaware that the Mississippi proceeding should take precedence. Delta Pine was the wronged party, and its lawsuit was filed first and should go first. The judge agreed and granted Delta Pine's motion. The Delaware suit was put on hold; the Mississippi case would proceed. The lawsuit with the largest demand for actual damages in Mississippi history, more than a billion dollars, would be litigated in one of the poorest counties in America.

The hearing in Mississippi before Circuit Judge Elzy Smith did not go as well for Delta Pine. Allen again presented an eloquent argument, but he couldn't seem to get through to the judge. As the hearing progressed, Michael de Leeuw, who was a senior associate at Fried Frank and became my dear friend, realized the problem: Judge Smith couldn't understand a word Allen was saying. Allen was a smart guy—he graduated *magna cum laude* from Harvard Law School—but he was a New Yorker to the core, even more than Tim Herlihy. Allen and the judge had but one habit of speech in common: Neither pronounced the r at the end of words. Allen, who didn't lack for confidence, often said he worked only on "big mattas." The judge, who couldn't decipher what Allen was saying, asked him more than once, "Mr. Kezsbom, why are we heah?"

Two classic movies, *Cool Hand Luke* and *My Cousin Vinny*, come to mind. To quote Strother Martin in the former, Judge Smith and Allen had "a failure to communicate." There was a similar failure in the latter. Judge Chamberlain Haller, played by Fred Gwynne, was mystified when Joe Pesci's Vinny Gambini referred to the young defendants as "the two yutes." The real judge in Clarksdale was just as befuddled as the fictional one in the movie. On the way home, Michael convinced Allen they needed to hire a lawyer Judge Smith could understand.

I became that lawyer, and the opportunity came at a good time. The Mississippi Chemical case was over, and my case against Volvo might never pay off. Ingalls wasn't getting sued as often, and my plate was far from full. I needed the work, and the work came. It wasn't an Ingalls matter, but it came to me thanks to an Ingalls matter. I had worked on the DAP grand jury investigation with Dick Sauber, an excellent white-collar lawyer at Fried Frank who later served as special counsel to President Biden. When Allen and Michael started looking for a Mississippi litigator, Dick, whose real name is Dick, recommended me, and I was soon on board. Judge Smith retired before he conducted any more hearings, but he could have understood every word I said.

Corpse or Client?

W orking on the case was a wonderful experience. I had an opportunity to litigate with and against excellent lawyers at Fried Frank, our co-counsel at Boies, Schiller & Flexner, and our principal opposition, Kirkland & Ellis. I made many trips to New York and took depositions all over the country. I spent time in Kirkland's offices in Chicago, New York, Washington, and San Francisco. I deposed several witnesses in St. Louis, including Monsanto's CEO, who in all candor was lacking in candor.

Partners in big New York firms enjoy very comfortable incomes in large measure because the firms have far more associates than partners. Leverage is the key. Consistent with New York staffing practices, Fried Frank assembled a large team of bright but mostly inexperienced associates to work on the Delta Pine case.

I recall several anecdotes resulting from the firm's staffing. When I was about to begin taking depositions, I met in New York with the Fried Frank associates and was asked how I liked my deposition outlines prepared. I answered with two words: "by me." But that was not the New York way. Fried Frank associates prepared drafts that I edited and invariably shrunk to a fraction of their original size.

When I flew north to Chicago for my first deposition, the young associate who had prepared the outline flew west to attend. We rendezvoused at Midway and shared a cab to our hotel. She looked out the right side along the way and asked what that ocean was. "Not an ocean," I said, "Lake Michigan." I hoped she was better at law than geography.

Two or three years later, while the case was in high gear, we had a team meeting at Fried Frank's offices in New York. Delta Pine CEO Tom Jagodinski, known to one and all as Jag, attended. By then, Jag had grown accustomed to both the pros and cons of New York staffing. No stone was left unturned, but turning over all the stones didn't come cheap.

We took a break, and everyone left the conference room except Jag and me. I studied an interesting piece of art on the wall, a black-and-white photograph with low-angle lighting. It featured a man in a suit lying on the floor in an office building. I asked Jag if he knew what the photo was supposed to represent, if the man was supposed to be dead. Acerbic and quick, Jag answered immediately: "Nah," he said. "That's a Fried Frank client who just opened the bill."

Brain Boxwood

The two members of the Fried Frank team to whom I became closest were Michael and Rachel Amamoo a/k/a the Moo, who were even more different on the surface than Abid and Jimmie and Monsanto and Delta Pine. Michael is a big white guy from New Jersey, the Moo a small black woman from South Australia. But below the surface, the two had a great deal in common. Both were very bright and able. Both were fine writers and loved to write. And both were very funny. Michael had written pieces for *The Onion*.

Rachel was beautiful and exotic when I last saw her. Think Halle Berry looks, Nicole Kidman accent. It's been twenty years, but I'm sure she still is. She left Fried Frank before the case ended and moved to London with her boyfriend Phil, also an Aussie, to practice law there. They had started dating in New York and raced together in the New York City Marathon. Phil collapsed and nearly died, Rachel nursed him back to health, and their commitment to each other grew. After a short stint in London, they quit their jobs and spent many months on a long overland journey up the continent of Africa from Johannesburg to Cairo. The trip could have ended their relationship but cemented it instead. They returned to Australia, married, and have three sons.

Michael and I stay in touch and see each other whenever we can. He became a partner at Fried Frank but left to join the firm of Cozen O'Connor, where he's the vice-chair of business litigation. Several years ago, I volunteered to help him prepare for an oral argument in the United States Supreme Court. He won the case five to four.

My small favor for Michael is nothing compared to what he's done for me. He has very generously reviewed and improved the manuscripts of all five of my previous books. I'm sure he would help me again with this one even if I weren't writing nice things about him.

When the Moo came to Jackson to work on the Delta Pine case, the runners at Brunini would stand in line for a chance to pick her up at the airport and take her back when the time came. On one trip, she came to observe a deposition I was defending. The witness, who was bright and accomplished, needed no assistance in dealing with the questions from Monsanto's lawyer. I rarely objected and listened with one ear as Rachel and I entertained ourselves by writing a story on her legal pad. She would write one sentence, and I would write the next. Try it sometime; it's fun.

Speaking of one ear, I looked over at the witness at one point and saw something I hadn't noticed before, something that shocked me. But though I was shocked, I pride myself on keeping a poker face, and I kept one then. It was my turn in our alternating-sentence story, but instead of a sentence I wrote a single word: "Ear." Rachel gave me a curious look, which I answered with the poker face. It was now her turn, and she wrote: "?" I added two clues: "His right ear." She gave me the same look, so I added a nonverbal clue. I tilted my head to the left, toward the witness. She followed the clue with her eyes, but I kept looking at her. Unlike me, she did not keep a poker face. She looked like she'd just seen Freddy Krueger.

From the witness's right ear canal, a remarkably luxuriant growth of hair sprouted. The dense hair curled up and out. A gray boxwood that was long overdue for pruning appeared to be growing out of his brain. I'd never seen anything like it, though I suppose there was another ear just like it on the left side of his head. I decided the witness's wife was either blind or didn't care. There's no way Carrie would let me leave the house looking like that.

After the Moo regained her composure, we returned to the short story, which now took on an auditory theme. The drama over, the deposition continued, and our witness did an excellent job. Despite his auricular shrubbery, he understood the questions far better than Judge Smith understood Allen.

Always Hang up the Phone

On one of my trips to New York, I arranged for Michael and me to have dinner with my law school classmate John Hardiman and his wife Donna. John was and remains the self-appointed and undisputed class clown of the Duke Law class of '82. Don't let him near a microphone unless you have time on your hands. He'll be playing here the rest of his life.

John is one of my buddies who goes on our annual Regression golf trip. He's a generous guy and has hosted us often at his vacation home on Sea Island. He's a partner at Sullivan & Cromwell, whose offices were in the building next to Fried Frank's. I knew an evening with John, Michael, and Donna would be entertaining, so I set it up.

After my meeting with the Fried Frank team ended for the day, I went down to meet John between the two buildings. Michael needed to stop by his office and told me he would be down shortly. I was dressed in business casual, but not John. He wore a custom suit and a beautiful tie. Great hair too. I asked if he always dressed that way, and he said he did. His biggest client, Goldman Sachs, had offices in the same building, and he met with them often. They dressed to the nines, so he did too.

Michael was taking a while, and I decided to make sure he knew where we were. My phone was dead, so I called him on John's. He didn't answer, so I left a message. Then John and I resumed our talk. He wanted to know if Fried Frank's lawyers wore suits to the office. Not even close, I said. Khakis and sport shirts were the best they could do. And they needed elastic waistbands, I told him, because they ate non-stop. There was a big tray of pastries in the morning, a huge spread for lunch, then cookies and brownies in the afternoon. Fried Frank was, I concluded, the "big, fat, sloppy firm."

Michael soon arrived, and we had a wonderful dinner with John and Donna. It was fun to introduce brilliant, funny friends to each other and sit back and listen. When the last of the wine was gone and Michael had finished his customary glass of grappa, it was time to head our separate ways. I was catching a cab to my hotel downtown, John and Donna were heading to their apartment on the Upper East Side, and Michael had arranged a car to take him across the Hudson to his home in New Jersey.

John and Donna left first, then Michael's car pulled up. I told him how much I enjoyed it, then confirmed the plan to resume our meeting in the morning at 9:30. After climbing into the back seat, just before closing the door, Michael smiled and said, "That's right, 9:30 at the big, fat, sloppy firm." He winked as the car pulled away.

I stood there on the sidewalk, alone and speechless. There had been lots of wine, so it took me a second, but it didn't take long. I had failed to hang up John's phone when I left the message. John and I kept talking, and Michael's phone kept recording.

When I walked into the conference room the next morning, I didn't know what to expect. But there sat Michael, a wide grin on his face. He'd had his fun and wasn't going to rub it in. I acknowledged with a nod that he'd played it well, and that was the end of it. To my knowledge, he never told his colleagues at Fried Frank. My recording faux pas, unlike Stu's, cost me nothing, and I learned a valuable lesson: Always make sure you hang up the phone.

Dick Must Die

The alternating sentences Rachel and I used to entertain our-selves during Mr. Boxwood's deposition were not the only stories we wrote during the Delta Pine years. Michael, the Moo, and I did plenty of legal writing, but we enjoyed creative writing too. We decided to have a short story contest and had so much fun the first time that we had two more. I know Michael won the first one ,and we had a three-way tie in the second. I don't remember who won the third, or if anyone did. Rachel was half a world away by then and, whatever the stakes may have been, it would have been hard for the winner to collect.

I've forgotten a lot about our contests, but I remember the topic of one and the stakes in another. As for the topic, one of the lawyers working on the case, whom I'll call Dick, was remarkably obnoxious and arrogant. You might think there would have been an army of obnoxious, arrogant lawyers in a huge case like this one, but Dick was in a class by himself. He was a blowhard's blowhard, a know-it-all's know-it-all, a dick's dick. Working with him was excruciating and invariably left the rest of us angry and exhausted.

We turned to strong drink but, when no drink was strong enough, decided to vent. We would have another short story contest and write our way out of our pain. The rules were simple. The plot of each entry was up to the author, but we all had to use the same title: "Dick Must Die."

I remember bits and pieces of my story. I wrote that several of the senior lawyers working on the case were commiserating about the misery of having to deal with Dick. How much better would our lives be if he were no longer around? Channeling Henry II, one of us asked, "Will no one rid us of this turbulent priest?"

A young Fried Frank associate overheard us and took us literally. He'd seen Dick in action and felt our pain. And he was ambitious; he wanted to get ahead in the firm. What better way, he decided, than to rid us of this turbulent priest. He hatched a foolproof plan and dispatched Dick with dispatch. The associate's future at the firm, he was certain, was now secure.

I remember the stakes in our first contest because I proposed them. Three judges, one chosen by each of us, would grade the stories. The grading would be blind. The contestants coming in second and third would take the winner out on the town in New York. We would wind up in a karaoke bar, where the contestant coming in last would kick off the festivities by singing a song chosen by the runner-up.

Michael won, I finished second, Rachel third. We scheduled the outing for my next trip to New York. Word spread, and several other members of the Fried Frank team joined us. In hopes of embarrassing Rachel, I chose a big, bold number for her, "Respect" by Aretha Franklin. But the Moo could sing, she could dance, and she was fearless. She sounded just like Aretha in *Blues Brothers*. The notion that I could embarrass her was embarrassing.

But the singing got worse, and the night got better. I recall two highlights. We encouraged another associate, Mark Dely, to take the mic, but he refused, citing his inability to sing. But we refused to let him refuse, kept goading, and beer and shame finally brought him around. When he started in on "New York, New York," we realized he'd been telling the gospel truth. He couldn't carry a tune in the world's largest bucket, and his version of the Sinatra classic was one for the ages. If he ever hit a single correct note, it was accidental. When I looked over at Michael, tears were streaming down his face.

Michael's a good singer, but he doesn't speak Japanese. That may seem irrelevant, but it proved to be an obstacle when it came to the last song of the night. Emboldened by drink, Michael decided to spin the dials on the karaoke machine and sing whatever song popped up, whether he knew it or not. When the dials came to a rest, he stared blankly at the machine, then broke out laughing. He didn't know the song, and he didn't know the language. He didn't even know the alphabet. But, undaunted, he hit the play button and spent the next three minutes doing his best to sound like a Japanese lounge singer. This time I was the one crying.

Johnny Thunder

Michael followed up his poor imitation of an Asian nightclub act by trying to perform another song he didn't know two or three years later. This time he appeared in Jackson and was accompanied by younger Fried Frank colleague Brian Howard. The performance must have been my idea. I was evidently there, and I'm told I introduced them, but I have no memory of any of it. It seems like something I would remember, but I don't. I can't blame it on a brain hemorrhage or Demerol this time, so I'll say I had too much to drink then or I'm too old now.

You may wonder how I know about the performance when I don't recall it. Here's how: On a Friday afternoon in March 2024, while making final edits to the manuscript for this book, I received an email from Michael. Attached to it was a story written by Brian about a night in a bar in Jackson, Mississippi, in the Year of Our Lord 2006. I read the entertaining story, contacted Michael, and he confirmed that it was true. What follows is my take on Brian's take on a memorable night in Jackson that I don't remember.

First, some background, and this part I do remember: The Pates —father Kelly and son Andrew—were my favorite local band. Great guys and fabulous musicians. Kelly was a gifted acoustic guitarist, young Andrew a keyboard prodigy. My fingers couldn't move that fast if they didn't have to hit where I aimed them. They were both talented vocalists and had a long playlist of great songs. I kept up with their schedule and went to see them whenever I could. When they played at Ann Lowrey's wedding reception, I mounted the stage, sang "The Weight" by The Band, and took a load off Fannie. I was a Pates groupie.

Now for the part I don't recall: It so happened that the Pates were playing on a night Michael and Brian were coming to town on Delta Pine business. I knew Michael and Brian were also musicians. Michael was a guitarist, Brian a keyboardist. I must have put two and two together and decided my New York friends should play during a break between sets by my Mississippi friends. It was a must. I would have cleared it with Kelly, who would have said bring 'em on.

I evidently thought it best to give the New Yorkers a heads-up and sent Michael an email, which he says he received while they were changing planes in Atlanta. Surely an hour-long flight would give them enough time to put together a short set list. But the task proved to be a challenge. They weren't sitting in the same row, they had never played together, and they didn't play the same kind of music. They exchanged lists of songs they knew. One song, but only one, was on both. It was "American Girl" by Tom Petty. Easy to play, easy to sing. If push came to shove, they could pull it off.

Michael also passed Brian a chart of chord progressions for another song, "Johnny Thunder" by the Kinks. Michael had recently discovered the song and loved it, but it was not a credible candidate for their short show in Jackson. It was hard to play and hard to sing, and Brian had never heard it, much less played it. He listened to it twice on his earphones and gave up.

When they arrived at the venue, the place was packed. In his story, Brian claims there were 200–300 people there, though I don't recall a local watering hole that held that many. Having no memory of the night, I shouldn't question Brian's, but I suspect the embarrassment he soon experienced has caused his mind to exaggerate the crowd size in the nearly two decades since then.

He and Michael got drinks to start catching up with me and listened to the Pates. These weren't a couple of local yokels. They were virtuosos. Brian was mesmerized by Andrew on the keys. He was as good as anyone Brian had ever seen, at the Kennedy Center or anywhere else. They got more drinks. Why not? There was no way they were going to follow these guys. According to Brian, when Michael told me they weren't going to play, I just grinned and shook my head. I had a plan; I must have.

When the band took a break, my plan unfolded. Andrew invited me up to the stage before leaving it. I took the mic and announced to the crowd that we were in for a special treat. Two fine musicians, friends of mine, had just flown in from the place so nice they named it twice, the one and only New York, New York. I asked the crowd to give it up for Michael and Brian.

And the crowd, filled with more Pates groupies, gave it up. My buddies could have cut and run, but that would have been poor form, especially for two of New York's finest. As Mark Dely reminded us with his unforgettable performance of "New York, New York" in New York, New York, if you can make it there, you can make it anywhere. And surely they could make it here. Michael and Brian mounted the stage. Hot lights shone down on their sweaty brows. How could this be happening?

But things started to look up. They performed "American Girl," and it went well. Easy to play, easy to sing, and they both knew it cold. Michael sang lead, and Brian added the background vocal— "make it last all night." They closed to a rousing ovation and whoops from the crowd. They weren't as good as Kelly and Andrew, but they weren't supposed to be. They were lawyers.

Brian stood up, smiled, and breathed a sigh of relief. He had survived his three minutes of Mississippi fame and was ready to disappear back into the crowd. But Michael, being Michael, had other ideas. He whispered "Johnny Thunder" to Brian and nodded for him to place the crumpled handwritten chord progression on the music stand. Brian couldn't believe it. They were really going to play a song he'd heard for the first time two hours earlier and had never played? Surely not. But there was no stopping Michael now. He played the opening chord, a D, then looked at Brian. What was he to do? He played a D.

It was the one and only note they played in common. Michael hardly knew the song, and Brian didn't know it at all. When he realized they were playing different songs neither of them knew, Brian resorted to the musical equivalent of the Hippocratic Oath. He turned the volume of his keys all the way down. As he sat there playing the equivalent of air keyboard, he noticed Andrew,

Mississippi's Beethoven, standing in front of him, watching his hands but hearing nothing. After sixty seconds, Michael recognized his mistake and gave up in mid-line. The sound just trailed off. In his story, Brian called it The Longest Minute in the History of Music. The crowd's response was not as warm this time.

Michael's memory of the night is far less traumatic than Brian's. That doesn't surprise me. After all, Michael's the guy who sang a karaoke song in Japanese. He doesn't deny the "Johnny Thunder" meltdown but recalls that they redeemed themselves with a decent cover of "Thunder Road" before leaving the stage.

Thanks for this story go to Ray Davies of the Kinks, who wrote "Johnny Thunder," to Brian Howard, who wrote a story about a memorable night on what was his first and only trip to Mississippi, and to Michael, who passed Brian's story along to me. I must have seen Brian for the very last time that night. I wish I could remember it. Sounds like I had a fabulous time.

Good-Looking Burga (Not Burqa)

I traveled to Delta Pine's headquarters in Scott only once in my four years of working on the case. The purpose of the trip was to attend a Delta Pine board of directors meeting. Allen would brief the board members on the status of the litigation, and they would get to speak to the lawyers handling the biggest case in the company's history. Though not for the reasons you might expect, it was another memorable night, and this one I remember.

The meeting was held in Scott in a one-room cabin with a large stone fireplace at one end. Dinner was a Southern fried buffet featuring catfish and chicken. One of the board members, with an accent that matched Allen's, poked at something round on one of the trays. "Hushpuppy," I said. He gave me an odd look. I explained what hushpuppies were and said they were good. He didn't bite.

Not long after Allen began his presentation, we were besieged by winged trespassers. Mosquitoes came swarming down the chimney into the room, which was filled with potential victims. Jag, our host, didn't take the invasion lying down. Armed with nothing but bug spray, he joined battle, circling the room, going from bug to bug, and blasting away. His aim was true, and the body count mounted. I tried to listen to Allen—we all did—but I already knew the status of the case. What I didn't know was how the battle between Jag and the army of mosquitoes would turn out. How long would they keep coming? What if Jag ran out of spray? Was there not a damper on the fireplace he could close? How would the drama end? It ended when Allen ended his spiel, we said our goodbyes, and left.

We climbed into a minivan rental, with Allen at the wheel, and headed south to Greenville, where we were staying. The night was still young, and Michael was in no mood to call it quits. He wanted to gamble, specifically to shoot craps. We parked and walked to a riverboat casino anchored on the bank of the Big Muddy. It was a Wednesday night, the place nearly empty, but Michael found one craps table open for business. It was occupied by the croupier and a lonely man who was apparently not gambling. He rolled but didn't bet. Michael bet but didn't roll. They were allies against the house. The man rolled winners over and over for Michael, whose stack of chips grew while Allen and I talked.

Jag had recently broken the news to Allen that I would be lead counsel at trial. I hadn't lobbied for the job, which Allen knew, and he understood the need to have a Mississippi lawyer for a Mississippi jury. But he was still disappointed. He told me he would be comfortable trying a case in any court in America. But, I thought, the Circuit Court in Rosedale wasn't just any court in America. I wasn't sure I was local enough to try a case there, but I was sure Allen wasn't. Putting a New York lawyer in charge would give up much of the home-field advantage Delta Pine had worked so hard to achieve.

Unlike most gamblers, Michael quit while he was ahead. He tossed a twenty-dollar chip to his friend the roller, cashed in the rest, and the three of us walked out into the night. On our stroll back to the minivan, Allen made a surprising announcement: He was hungry. I wondered how that could be. We'd feasted on an all-you-can-eat buffet not three hours earlier. But maybe Allen was too busy preparing his presentation to eat very much. Or maybe, as a Fried Frank lawyer, he was used to eating at frequent intervals, and it was time to eat again.

Whatever the reason, Allen was hungry, and he had a plan. We would go to Doe's Eat Place, a longstanding Delta institution, and he would order a big steak. But Michael rained on his parade and said it was closed. "Why?" asked Allen. Because it's ten o'clock on Wednesday night, Michael pointed out. "So?" Allen asked. He really was New York through and through. He demanded proof, so we headed to the restaurant. The lights were off, the place empty. Just as Tim Herlihy couldn't ride the subway in Jackson, Allen couldn't order a steak in Greenville after ten on a weeknight.

But Allen was still hungry, and he wasn't giving up. We returned to the minivan, again with Allen at the helm, and began a search. Late-night offerings in Greenville were limited, but we soon saw a familiar sign. There was a Wendy's ahead on the left with the lights on. As we approached, Allen said that Fried Frank represented Wendy's, but of course only in "the big mattas." He pulled into the drive-thru lane and admired the two-dimensional plastic cheeseburger on the sign. "That's a good-looking burga," he said. Like matta, no r at the end. Man, I thought, he really is hungry.

But though this was supposed to be fast food, Allen wasn't eating anytime soon. When it came time to place his order, he had a harder time than when I was looking for Germaine's. The first obstacle was the language barrier. Allen and the woman on the speaker both spoke English, but it wasn't the same version. Like Elzy Smith, she couldn't understand a word he said. And that wasn't all. Fried Frank may have represented Wendy's, but I don't believe Allen had ever eaten at one. He didn't know the lingo and didn't order a single, double, or triple. Instead, he said he wanted "a burga." He might as well have ordered two yutes.

When two people can't understand each other and a third understands both, it's human nature for the one witnessing the difficulty to intervene and help. Take Barbara Billingsley, for example, who came to the rescue of the passengers and flight attendant in *Airplane*. Because she spoke both English and jive, she was able to translate and help them overcome their failure to communicate.

From my perch in the back seat, I was in a position much like Barbara's. Not only could I understand the two accents, but I spoke fluent Wendy's, having dined there more times than I would care to admit to my cardiologist. I started to speak up and help sort things out, but then I stopped myself. It would be a test. If Allen could order a cheeseburger in Greenville, maybe he could try a case in Rosedale. I also figured he and the woman would eventually work it out, and listening would be fun.

It took a while, but at long last they succeeded. By the time they finally reached a meeting of the minds, Michael had decided he was hungry too. It's no wonder; Allen and the woman had been talking about food for five minutes. When Michael ordered his own meal, it took no more than ten seconds. Maybe he could try the case with me in Rosedale. I debated getting a Frosty but was still full from dinner number one. We pulled into a spot in the Wendy's parking lot, and I watched as Allen and Michael ate dinner number two. I was envious; those really were some good-looking burgas.

Ch-Ch-Ch-Ch-Changes

The turn of the century brought changes and growing pains to the legal profession in Mississippi and the big law firms in Jackson. Business was excellent, primarily because of mass-tort litigation. Plaintiffs' lawyers signed up clients from all over America and filed suits in the counties along the Mississippi River that were known for their plaintiff-friendly judges and juries. Based on Mississippi's liberal joinder rules, thousands of plaintiffs who lived thousands of miles apart and had never met each other could join together in a single lawsuit. In Jefferson County, one of the lawyers' favorites, there were far more plaintiffs with pending cases than there were residents of the county. Manufacturers of products containing asbestos and silica were favorite targets, but there were others as well.

The big Jackson firms, which were hired to defend the cases, grew and prospered. In just a few years, the number of lawyers in the litigation department I chaired at Brunini doubled, the number of paralegals tripled, and the revenues we generated increased dramatically. And though I was in charge, I had nothing to do with it. It was all the market, and the market was great.

Regional firms saw an opportunity, opened offices in Jackson, and began recruiting partners from Jackson firms to join them. Groups split off from established firms when they saw they could make far more with a specialized mass-tort practice. A lawyer who recruited me when I was in law school started a firm with three colleagues, and he now owns a winery in Sonoma Valley. Back in the day, Mississippi lawyers were lucky if they could afford a bottle of wine from Sonoma.

We prospered at Brunini, but success came with challenges. Our compensation system was still based primarily on seniority, and that was, to use a phrase that is now in vogue, no longer sustainable. I suspect that our most productive litigators were offered big increases in compensation to leave and join regional firms, and we didn't want to lose them. Change was coming, and it was inevitable. The question was how to accomplish it.

In my judgment, the firm didn't accomplish the change as well as it could have. The number of people who served on the board and made compensation decisions was reduced significantly, and the small group made big changes with little input from the rest of us. The changes didn't have much effect on me, at least financially. Some of our lawyers made more and some less, but my compensation remained about the same. But I didn't like how the change was made, and because I was a confident litigator and thought I should be the one presenting the case, I became the spokesman for the loyal opposition. It was a stressful time.

And during that stressful time, I was contacted by a headhunter working for McGlinchey Stafford. They were looking to add an experienced litigator in their Jackson office, and we began a tentative courtship. I liked the lawyers in the firm, especially Jerry Johnson, the managing partner in Jackson. He led the effort to recruit me, and I ultimately decided it was time to make a move. It was a painful and emotional decision—the Brunini firm was like family to me, and I always thought I'd spend my entire career there—but I needed a change and a fresh start. In an act of kindness that I'll never forget, Granville Tate, one of my friends at Brunini, graciously hosted a cocktail party for me after my last day at the firm.

Ingalls, Delta Pine, and other clients followed me to McGlinchey, and I enjoyed my time there, but it didn't last. After I'd been at the firm eight or nine months, I stopped by Jerry's office one day to tell him a friend at Brunini might be interested in joining us. He asked me to come into his office and close the door. He had some news that preempted mine. Baker Donelson, a large regional firm with a big Jackson office, had initiated talks with a group from McGlinchey. Half the lawyers in the office, including Jerry and me, were ultimately invited to join Baker.

I was prepared to change firms for the second time in a year, but then I found out that Baker did work for Monsanto. If I joined the firm, I would have to give up the Delta Pine case. Not only would that have been a terrible disappointment—I was slated to be lead trial counsel in what would arguably be the biggest case ever tried in Mississippi—but it would have been wrong. Delta Pine and Fried Frank had been very good to me, and I couldn't abandon them. I told Baker Donelson and Jerry that I had to stay behind.

Poor Jerry felt awful. He had wooed me away from my firm of more than two decades, but now his whole practice group was leaving and he had no choice but to leave with them. He left me a sad voicemail telling me of his decision while he and his accomplished wife Louisa were in New England visiting colleges with their son. I called him back and said he sounded like he needed to call the suicide hotline. I told him not to feel bad. He could be the guinea pig, find out if Baker was a good place to work, and I could reevaluate when the Delta Pine case ended. Though at times it doesn't seem like it, all cases must end.

And in late 2006, the Delta Pine case finally did. After courting, agreeing to marry, then going through a bitter, expensive breakup, Delta Pine and Monsanto let bygones be bygones and got back together. Monsanto again agreed to acquire Delta Pine, this time for $1.5 billion in cash, and this time the deal went through. The two companies reunited, and it felt so good.

After the settlement was made public, Baker Donelson again came calling. I was happy at McGlinchey and reluctant to leave, but I was ultimately persuaded by staffing considerations. Baker had a much bigger Jackson office and far more good young litigators, and I would need them on an Ingalls matter that had become very busy. I had never thought I would change firms a single time, but in February 2007 I changed for the second time in less than two years. A handful of people I worked with made the change with me, including my secretary, two associates, and two paralegals. Ann Lowrey was one of them. She was planning to go to law school but decided against it based on her experience working with me. I wonder what I would have done if I'd worked at a law firm before I went to Duke. That, like many things, I'll never know.

Pre- Pre- Pre-Call

The Ingalls matter on which I was busy was already six years old when I arrived at Baker Donelson. I would now be defending it with my third team in my third firm. The litigation already had a long, complex procedural history. The basic allegations—racial discrimination in promotions and a racially hostile work environment—hadn't changed, but the litigation had gone from one enormous case to ninety much smaller ones.

The case began in 2001 when I was at Brunini. It was filed as a class action in federal court in Biloxi by eleven black employees and an unincorporated association that called itself Ingalls Workers for Justice, IWFJ for short. We did not respond to the plaintiffs' complaint with an answer but instead filed a motion to dismiss the class-action claims and various other claims and parties. Our principal argument, drafted by Steve Allen, was that the claims of each member of the proposed class would depend on highly individualized facts. As a result, the case was unsuitable for litigation as a class action.

The case was assigned to Judge Gex. When he did not rule on our motion promptly, the plaintiffs' lawyers—a handful from a public-interest firm in California assisted by Mississippi counsel from the Delta—became impatient. They first made a direct appeal to Judge Gex and asked him to rule right away. When that didn't spur him to action, they wrote a letter complaining about the delay to Judge Wingate, who was the Chief Judge of the Southern District at the time. I suppose they didn't know that Judge Wingate had a reputation for being slower to rule on motions than Judge Gex. No matter what they knew or didn't know, their complaint to the chief judge about the judge handling the case struck me as unwise.

Judge Gex ultimately granted our motion and dismissed the class and other claims. I believe the plaintiffs' lawyers tried to take an immediate appeal to the Fifth Circuit, but I could be wrong. They tried to take several appeals in mid-case, including two to the United States Supreme Court. They litigated the case as if they had an unlimited budget. In any event, the ruling stood, and the case was no longer a class action. The court gave other black employees an opportunity to intervene as plaintiffs, and approximately 200 did so, though more than half later dropped out. We wound up with ninety plaintiffs.

The powers that be changed the federal rules in the 1990s to require courts to conduct an early case management conference with the attorneys in every case. The primary purpose of the conference, which was ordinarily conducted by phone, was to set a schedule to take the case from beginning to end. The rules also directed the attorneys to confer before the conference to discuss a proposed schedule and other issues.

After the court scheduled our case management conference, the delightful legal assistant for the plaintiffs' Mississippi lawyers called me. She didn't want to schedule the attorney conference required by the rules but instead wanted to schedule a call for the attorneys to discuss the matters that needed to be discussed in the required attorney conference. When I realized what she wanted, we had an exchange that went something like this:

Me: Under the rules, the attorneys are required to have a pre-call before the case-management-conference call with the judge.

Her: That's right.

Me: And the lawyers on your side want to have a pre-pre-call to discuss what we need to talk about on the pre-call.

Her: I guess so.

Me: So what is it we're having now?

Her: What do you mean?

Me: Is this the pre-pre-pre-call?

Her (laughing): I suppose it is.

We had all the calls, discovery began, and the parties exchanged written requests. True to form, the plaintiffs' lawyers wanted virtually every document in the shipyard. One of their requests was for all documents relating to Ingalls' contracts with the U.S. government and ships built for the Navy. Nearly all of Ingalls' contracts are with the government, and nearly all the ships it builds are for the Navy. We never knew how many millions of documents were covered by the request, though the vast majority had no conceivable relevance to the plaintiffs' claims. We objected to the requests and tried to resolve the dispute amicably, but we didn't come close. When our efforts failed, the plaintiffs filed a motion to compel us to produce everything they wanted.

The motion, which was a hundred pages long, arrived while I was in Colorado on a family vacation. Katie Gilchrist, who had begun working on the case, called to tell me about it. I asked her to contact plaintiffs' lead counsel, whom I'll call Dick, tell him where I was, and secure his agreement to a two-week extension. That would give us a total of four weeks to respond. She soon called me back. To my surprise—though I shouldn't have been surprised—Dick had refused.

His refusal, like the complaint to Judge Wingate about Judge Gex, struck me as unwise. I decided to email him and not copy anyone else on either team. It would just be the two of us. I told him we had a long, hard fight ahead, and we would all be better off if we accommodated each other's reasonable requests and fought only about issues that really mattered. If they didn't agree to the extension, I said we would file a one-page motion for an extension, cite my vacation and their hundred pages, and the court would undoubtedly grant it. I asked him to reconsider. Once again, again unwisely, he refused. We filed the one-page motion, and the court granted it without waiting for a response.

After I returned from Colorado, Katie and I prepared a response to the motion to compel and filed it on the extended deadline. A week or so later, my phone rang. It was Dick. He sounded sheepish. It was a call he undoubtedly didn't want to make but, to his credit, he made it. He didn't chicken out with an email. They needed an extension for their reply brief on their motion, he said.

I was tempted to remind Dick that he had refused our request for an extension so I was refusing his, but doing so would have been unwise as well as unprofessional. Playing tit for tat would invite more pettiness, and the judge would have granted the plaintiffs' request for an extension and rolled his eyes at me for not consenting to it. I told Dick I wanted him to remember the call, then said we had no objection. He thanked me, but he did not remember. Difficulties with Dick lasted as long as the litigation, and the litigation lasted more than a decade.

The ETW Team

We took the depositions of the plaintiffs while I was at McGlinchey. I shared responsibility for taking them with colleagues Tim Lindsay and Steve Brandon. Steve was an amateur astronomer. He bought a large telescope and took delivery of it while we were on the Coast. After dinner one night, we rolled it out onto a golf course, Steve focused it, and we saw Saturn and its rings.

The depositions revealed that the quality of the plaintiffs' claims varied widely. Several were excellent employees who probably should have been offered an opportunity to advance into management. Others were lousy employees who probably should have been discharged years earlier. Most fell somewhere in the middle. Some of the plaintiffs were credible witnesses, but we concluded that others were not credible and their claims had no merit.

If all the plaintiffs' claims were tried together, we feared they would benefit from strength in numbers, the differences would be blurred, and the strong plaintiffs would lift the weak, just as Margie Berryhill's case had lifted Frederick Bolian's in my nursing home days. We also knew there was no way a jury could possibly keep up with all the facts about ninety plaintiffs. Citing the risks of unfair prejudice and confusion, we filed a motion to sever the one case with ninety plaintiffs into ninety separate cases with one plaintiff apiece. Hoping for strength in numbers, the plaintiffs' lawyers opposed the motion, but the court granted it in late 2006.

And that was the state of play when I joined Baker Donelson in February 2007. The cases were soon reassigned to a new federal district judge, Sul Ozerden. Approximately fifteen of the cases were placed on each of six of his trial calendars. If the schedule remained in place, the last trials would take place nearly two years after the first ones.

Every case on the same calendar had the same deadlines for summary judgment motions and other pretrial tasks. Completing discovery and filing summary judgment motions in fifteen cases at the same time would be a monumental undertaking, and we would have to do it all again in fifteen more cases in just a few months, when trials of the cases on the previous calendar might be underway.

We needed a large, committed team to handle the mountain of work and, to my great relief, I was able to assemble one at Baker Donelson. Many of the firm's lawyers worked on the cases. Most did a fine job, but not all. One associate shirked her responsibility for drafting summary judgment briefs so completely that I had to spend a weekend rewriting her first brief and, weeks later, two other members of the team stayed up all night rewriting her second. She was not asked to draft a third.

But the core members of the team, the lawyers and paralegals who did the lion's share of the work, were all talented, hard-working, and reliable. And every one of them had a good sense of humor, which was crucial when you work as hard and spend as much time together as we did. The team included three members who came with me from McGlinchey, associate Adam Gates and paralegals Amy Schelver and Ann Lowrey. Four Baker Donelson lawyers joined us, shareholders Davis Frye and Scott Pedigo and associates Ceejaye Peters and Brandon Jolly. Leading such a fine group of professionals was a high point of my career.

When major league baseball teams trade players, there is often a "player to be named later," a throw-in to make the deal even out. At least that used to be the case. I recruited Adam Gates when he was in law school. He graduated in 2006 and immediately began working on the IWFJ litigation. When I decided to join Baker Donelson in February 2007, he'd been practicing law for less than a year. He was a prospect with potential, not a proven commodity. He was the player to be named later. Nearly fifteen years later, when Adam decided to join Watkins & Eager, I agreed to tag along. He was an accomplished litigator by then, and I was winding down with an eye on retirement. I was the player to be named later.

Adam was a newlywed when I recruited him but now has five children and more gray hair than I do. He's taken a prized object with him from firm to firm to firm. The object is a coffee cup he came across while we were at McGlinchey. When he packed up his things in 2007 to move to Baker Donelson, he took the cup with him, and when he packed again to join Watkins & Eager in late 2020, the cup went with him again. In January 2024, when I made a rare trip to the office three days before I typed these words, I spotted the cup on a shelf in his bookcase.

The coffee cup, provenance unknown, is decorated with the words "Expect to Win." Adam christened our team on the IWFJ litigation at Baker Donelson the Expect to Win team, ETW for short, and we expected to win.

Ronald McDonald, Esquire

Long before the ETW team was even a twinkle in my eye, I read an article in *Southern Living* about Gulf Hills Hotel & Resort in Ocean Springs. Gulf Hills has a fascinating history. Many believe the resort, which opened in 1927, was developed for the pleasure of Al Capone. You'll be shocked to learn there was drinking there during prohibition, purportedly gambling and prostitution as well. Elvis Presley became a frequent guest in the 1950s. He played the piano in The Pink Pony, the resort's lounge, and enjoyed the privacy. I made a mental note to give Gulf Hills a try when I traveled to the Coast on Ingalls business.

The opportunity came when depositions in the IWFJ litigation resumed six months after Hurricane Katrina ravaged the Gulf Coast. Many hotels were still closed, but not Gulf Hills, which is perched on a point high above the water. My colleagues and I stayed there many times and took depositions in the hotel's conference rooms.

Gulf Hills suited me to a tee. It wasn't fancy, but it was convenient, the rooms were nice, and I liked the continental breakfast. And the staff was friendly. Walking into the lobby was like walking into the bar in *Cheers*. Everybody knew my name. The hotel was on a golf course and surrounded by a residential neighborhood that was ideal for my morning walks. My regular route took me to a peninsula on Biloxi Bay where several people died in the hurricane. Only slabs remained where fine homes had stood not long before.

Soon after I joined Baker Donelson, we engaged Pete Rowland's firm to assemble focus groups to help us evaluate two very different pieces of litigation we were defending for Ingalls, the IWFJ cases and a suit brought by a company called Searex involving the construction of offshore rigs. We held the focus groups at Gulf Hills on consecutive days, for the Searex case on the first day and the IWFJ cases on the second. Pete's firm hired members of the public to serve as faux jurors. Lawyers on the ETW team split up, with one side representing Ingalls and the other representing the plaintiffs. The goal was to evaluate the company's exposure and identify our strengths and weaknesses. We presented the arguments of both sides, then watched the groups deliberate via closed circuit cameras.

I represented Searex the first day and watched the deliberations with mixed emotions. One side of me wanted the shipyard's arguments to prevail, but the other side—the competitive side—wanted to win. I swapped sides the next day and, along with Scott, represented the shipyard. To present the plaintiffs' arguments, Davis teamed up with Tiffanee Wade-Henderson, a fine and funny lawyer who was at Baker then and is Associate General Counsel at International Paper now. We learned from the focus groups that we might lose some of the IWFJ cases, but juries were unlikely to award significant damages. We also confirmed that trying the cases together would have dramatically increased the risk and that we had done the right thing by filing a motion to sever the cases.

Watching the focus groups deliberate was informative, entertaining and, at times, humiliating. Three members of the ETW team acquired short-lived nicknames from the faux jurors. One of them repeatedly butchered Scott's last name and added a syllable to it. We adopted the mispronunciation and called him Pedaggio. A woman complained that I didn't move my mouth when I talked. I can't see myself when I talk, but there must be some truth to what she said. I've had a chipped front tooth since I was ten years old, and friends I've known all my life have never noticed. Adam claims the woman nicknamed me Lamb Chop for Shari Lewis's sock puppet. I don't recall that, and it would make more sense to name me for the ventriloquist who didn't move her mouth than for the puppet who did. But maybe Adam's right. If there's one painful lesson I learned during my long life in the law, it's that jurors, both real and faux, don't have to make sense.

The nickname with the most staying power was bestowed on Davis. He's an excellent lawyer and did a fine job in the focus group, but one woman, it's fair to say, was not impressed. If she needed a lawyer, she said, she would rather have Ronald McDonald than Davis. We dubbed him Ronnie, which he loved just as much as you might imagine. The nickname lasted for a while but then fell into disuse.

Not long before Adam and I left Baker Donelson for Watkins & Eager, Davis left Baker for Butler Snow, now the largest firm in Mississippi. I know many of Davis's colleagues at his new firm. After this book is published, my hope is that the nickname he was given in 2007 will come to their attention and Davis will become Ronnie again.

The ETW Team's Clients

W e not only had a great ETW team at Baker Donelson, but we also worked with great in-house lawyers. Northrop Grumman acquired Litton Industries, Ingalls' parent company, in 2001. I immediately began working with Allen Peters, a Northrop in-house lawyer in Los Angeles. Two years later, Allen told me Northrop wanted to hire another in-house lawyer to manage litigation for Ingalls and Avondale, a smaller shipyard owned by the company on the Mississippi River a few miles upstream from New Orleans. Allen wanted to know if I knew anyone who might be interested. One of my colleagues at Brunini recommended Judy Perry Martinez, an excellent lawyer in private practice at Simon Peragine in New Orleans. Judy flew to Los Angeles, impressed the Northrop team, they offered her the job, and she accepted. The day she started at Northrop, she began managing my Ingalls cases.

Two years later, because of the high volume of litigation the two shipyards were experiencing, Northrop decided to hire a second in-house lawyer. Judy turned to Tom Hamrick, her longtime friend and former colleague at Simon Peragine. Tom and Judy had worked closely at the firm, and they wanted to work together again. When Tom's secretary told his father one day that Tom was at a meeting in Pascagoula, Dr. Hamrick put two and two together and decided that Tom was joining Northrop. Ingalls was the biggest company in Pascagoula, Northrop owned Ingalls, and Judy was the one and only person who could get Tom to leave Simon Peragine. Three months after Katrina flooded New Orleans, like Monsanto and Delta Pine the following year, Judy and Tom reunited, and it felt so good. I reported to Judy and Tom on all my Ingalls cases, including the IWFJ litigation.

Even under the best of circumstances, litigation is very stressful. It's an adversary system, conflict is constant, and the fear of making mistakes and the risk of losing are never far from your mind. Difficult in-house lawyers add to the anxiety. Those who second-guess your decisions—Dick of Beverly, for example—make the job far more stressful, as do those who make lousy changes to your pleadings and fly-speck your bills.

But Judy and Tom were great clients. They were experienced litigators and gave sound advice. They were always supportive, and they never questioned our sizable bills. They knew how hard we were working. They were also enjoyable company and became my dear friends during our years of working together. They still are.

Judy has always been committed to professional and public service. She spent a year as a fellow at the Advanced Leadership Initiative at Harvard and was later elected to serve as the president of the American Bar Association. As for Tom, many men have been described as gentlemen and scholars, but Tom really is one. He knows more stuff about more stuff than anyone else I know. If you're curious about Teddy Roosevelt, old coins, or single-malt Scotch, Tom's your guy.

I worked closely with Judy until 2011, when Northrop Grumman spun off its shipyards into a new publicly traded company, Huntington Ingalls Industries. She remained with Northrop and accepted a position in northern Virginia, where she served as vice president and chief compliance officer until her retirement. After the spinoff, Tom changed companies but not duties. He took a position at Huntington Ingalls, where he continued to oversee litigation for the shipyard. I worked with him constantly until I stopped working altogether.

Judy and Tom, and the many other in-house lawyers I worked with on Ingalls matters—Bill Powers, George Simmerman, Bobby Ariatti, John Carlson, Linda Boozer, Allen Peters, Chad Boudreaux, Jeff Bauer, and others—were all very good to me in the three decades after Bill Powers hired me to handle the McCann case. Their loyalty to me is why I paid fifty bucks to be an inactive member of the Bar instead of retiring for good. If Ingalls ever needs my help again, I can come out of retirement without having to take and pass the Bar exam again. I'm willing to do a lot for my friends at Ingalls, but I'm not willing to take the Bar exam.

Culture Clash

Hundreds of depositions were taken in the IWFJ litigation. I've forgotten the names of most of the witnesses and nearly all of what they said, but one deposition stands out.

A woman I'll call Susie, one of the IWFJ plaintiffs' lawyers, was probably our favorite on their side. She was polite and respectful and had a good sense of humor. Major Matthew Leggett was polite and respectful too, but good manners were all they had in common. Well, good manners and clothes. They both wore men's clothes. And haircuts. They both had crewcuts. But that's where the similarities ended.

Major Leggett was a middle-aged black man who'd spent his entire life in the Deep South. He was a military veteran and a high-ranking officer in the security force at the shipyard. Susie was a young white woman from the North, a lawyer in the California public-interest firm, and an activist for transgender rights. She sought to establish that men and women have the right to use the restroom of the sex with which they identify. Major Leggett had no use for any such right. He used the men's room.

When Susie and Major Leggett arrived for her to take his deposition, they were both dressed like men, but they were not dressed alike. Major Leggett was wearing his security uniform, his name on a brass plate over his shirt pocket and a sidearm strapped to his belt. Susie had on a men's pinstripe suit, a starched white dress shirt, and wingtips. She was also wearing an Ace bandage under her shirt or some similar binding to decentuate her breasts. Her high voice was the only giveaway, but it didn't give away enough to Major Leggett.

Susie began the deposition with a litany of process questions about how a deposition works, the kind I considered a waste of time. Though I was defending the deposition, I paid no attention and checked my emails. I would tune in when Susie got to substance. After a few minutes, Susie turned to me and asked if we could go off the record. I looked up, surprised, and said sure. She turned back to the witness and spoke. Because she had good manners, she spoke with a tone of sympathy, not anger.

"Major Leggett," she said, "I've noticed you've been saying 'yes, sir' and 'no, sir' when you answer my questions. I know you didn't realize this, but I'm a woman." Major Leggett's eyes opened wide. He said not a word. I guess I should have said something to him before the deposition, but telling the witness the sex of the lawyer on the other side was never part of my prep outline.

Susie sought to put him at ease. "It's not your fault. It happens all the time. But if you don't mind, would you please call me ma'am instead of sir?"

Though Major Leggett had good manners too, he was still reeling from the revelation that the person sitting across the table from him was a woman. "Yes, sir," he said.

Settling Without Settling

After we briefed summary judgment motions in the cases on the first trial calendar but before any of them went to trial, Judge Roper conducted a settlement conference in all ninety cases. We had conflicting goals in evaluating whether and how to settle. Ingalls wanted to avoid the adverse publicity that would come from a jury finding that the shipyard discriminated against black employees in promotions or subjected them to a racially hostile work environment. There had already been press coverage, and cases we lost would no doubt generate more interest than cases we won. And there was no way we would win them all, so bad publicity was almost certain if we didn't settle. On the other hand, Ingalls was strongly opposed to paying even small amounts to settle meritless cases. Settling baseless claims would just encourage the filing of more lawsuits. As the largest employer in the state, Ingalls could face a deluge.

During the conference, someone—I suspect Judge Roper—made a proposal that would accommodate both of our concerns. We would resolve the cases through confidential arbitrations with a limit on the amount that could be awarded. Ingalls would pay only those plaintiffs found by a neutral arbitrator to have meritorious claims, and there would be no headlines and no TV coverage.

To our surprise, the plaintiffs' lawyers agreed. They had been waiting seven years for their first jury trials, and now they wouldn't have them. We initially demanded that all the plaintiffs agree to arbitrate as a condition of the settlement, but when some of them balked, we decided to arbitrate as many cases as we could and deal with the other ones later. We wound up with fourteen plaintiffs who opted out. Their cases were put on hold until the arbitrations of all the others were completed.

We agreed on two arbitrators, Walter Johnson of Jackson and Amy Totenberg of Atlanta, and arranged for the arbitrations to be conducted in the new federal courthouse in Gulfport. The first arbitration, in the summer of 2008, was conducted before both arbitrators and included evidence the parties believed was relevant to all the plaintiffs' claims. We then began arbitrating individual plaintiffs' claims before a single arbitrator. To achieve some measure of efficiency and still minimize confusion, we soon agreed with plaintiffs' counsel to have several plaintiffs in each arbitration, from two to six. We chose plaintiffs who worked in the same department and same location for the same arbitration.

We had twenty-five to thirty arbitrations altogether. We didn't win all the cases by any means, and there was definitely some baby-splitting, but we were satisfied with the outcomes for the most part. And the arbitrations gave us all, but especially the inexperienced associates on the ETW team, a great opportunity to improve our trial skills. We had no jury, and the arbitrators didn't wear robes, but otherwise the arbitrations were just like trials in federal court, with most of the fun but only a fraction of the stress. Young lawyers in big firms rarely get an opportunity to give openings and closings and examine witnesses in a federal courtroom, but Adam, Ceejaye, and Brandon got to do it all.

The Biggest of Cats, The Most Tangled of Webs

W hile I was writing this, more than half the members of the ETW team gathered for a reunion at our home in Madison to reminisce about old times and help me remember stories from our years together. Here are a few from the arbitrations.

In support of their hostile environment claims, many of the plaintiffs alleged they'd seen nooses in the shipyard. We took the claims with more than a grain of salt. Almost without exception, neither the plaintiffs nor anyone else made any complaint at the time of the alleged noose sightings. Some of the claims, we were confident from the testimony about them, were outright fabrications. Others likely involved embellishment, with ropes used for legitimate purposes in the distant past now characterized as nooses intended to intimidate black employees.

Two plaintiffs in one arbitration claimed they saw the same noose, but their stories could not be reconciled. One said the alleged noose was very large, the other that it was tiny. One said it was hanging from a rafter, the other that it was on a wall. In an effort to bolster their contradictory testimony, their lawyers called to the stand one of the opt-out plaintiffs. He testified he saw the same noose.

But unfortunately for the witness, neither he nor the plaintiffs' lawyers read the transcript of his deposition before the arbitration. Or maybe they just hoped I didn't. The witness testified unequivocally when he was deposed that he'd never seen a noose in the shipyard. The cross-examination was a piece of cake. When his arbitration testimony was exposed as a lie, he didn't quibble or try to defend himself. Instead, he broke down and cried. That wasn't my goal, but I counted it as a win.

We usually had two lawyers from the ETW team at each arbitration, one shareholder and one associate, but Adam and Ceejaye both worked with me on an arbitration with six plaintiffs. One of the six was a very large woman in both height and girth, but she didn't let her size affect her sense of style. When she walked into the courtroom on the first day, she was wearing a bold leopard-print pantsuit. All but her head, hands, and feet were covered in the markings of the fearsome predator. Adam looked around and saw her. Ceejaye, concentrating on preparation, did not. Adam looked at Ceejaye with a somber expression and offered a four-word assessment: "That's one big cat."

Ceejaye looked over her shoulder, spotted the big cat, and came undone. She put her head down while she tried to recover. Though she made little noise, the table shook. She avoided eye contact with Adam, and the shaking gradually subsided.

ETW team members made countless trips to the Coast, driving up and down Highway 49 from Jackson to Gulfport and back. Scott had a bad habit of checking his phone when he was behind the wheel. While he was looking at his messages, the car often drifted to the right and hit those strips that make that funny noise that tells you to pull back into the lane. They're called rumble strips, which I know because I just looked them up.

Anyway, Scott hit the rumble strips so often that we named the practice for him. Pedigo became a verb. Team members who hit the rumble strips were guilty of pedigoing. All of us probably did it at least once or twice, but nobody pedigoed (pediwent?) like Scott did.

Two of our memories from the arbitrations were of incidents involving our loved ones back home. Early one morning in January 2009,

Brandon and I were about to begin an arbitration in Gulfport. It would be our first time to arbitrate together. He was suited up, his game face on, and ready to rumble, but not by running off the side of the road. We were walking into the courthouse when his phone rang. It was his wife, Natalie. She had bad news. An intruder had broken into their home in Madison.

The trespasser was not a thief but a wild animal. A deer had leaped through the kitchen window, shattering it and barely missing the Jollys' toddler, who was sitting at the kitchen table minding her own business. The uninvited beast proceeded to wreck the house, leaving a trail of blood behind. Adding insult to injury, the deer went into the bathroom, closed the bathtub drain, turned on the water, and flooded the house. The animal obviously had a bone to pick with the Jollys, or perhaps with people in general.

A neighbor came to the rescue but was armed only with a rake. There were no leaves in the house, so Natalie called 911. A young deputy soon arrived and sized up the scene. Instead of herding the deer out the door and back into nature, he cornered it in the water closet and dispatched it with a single shot. Then, remembering the adage to waste not, want not, he asked Natalie, "Ma'am, you gonna want that meat?" She told him to take the deer, and he promised it would be used to feed the prisoners in the county jail. Whether the promise was kept is unknown.

As we all know, it's the most natural thing in the world for a loving mother to want fame and fortune for her child. And so it was with Natalie's mother. There was little potential for riches from the deer incident, but fame was a real possibility. After all, how often does a deer break into a home, close a bathtub drain, turn on the water, and flood the place? Not very, I'm confident.

Natalie's mom realized the news value of the story and did the obvious: She alerted WAPT, the ABC affiliate in Jackson. Reporters rushed to the scene and interviewed Natalie, the UPI picked up the story, and the tale of the rogue deer in Madison was splashed across the front page of MSNBC's website by noon. Thanks to the deer and her mom, Natalie achieved her fifteen minutes of fame.

But what about Brandon? His home was a wreck, and his phone was pinging every fifteen seconds. Did he lose focus on the task at hand? He did not. Did his performance in the arbitration suffer? It did not. He pressed on, and we were victorious.

The second memory involved a loved one of mine. The best things in life are often unplanned. Ann Lowrey's firstborn, Ada Brooks, is one of them. She was born during the summer between Ann Lowrey's sophomore and junior years at Ole Miss and is a blessing to all who know her. Ann Lowrey's second child, Eason, was born in March 2007, a month after she and I joined Baker Donelson. He is now almost seventeen and at least four inches taller than the short little pipeline lawyer.

Ann Lowrey left Baker Donelson in the fall of 2008. Before then, she worked hard on the IWFJ litigation and the arbitrations. She was a valuable member of the ETW team and spent time with the plaintiffs' lawyers as well as the arbitrators.

Five months after the deer incident, on June 18, 2009, I was in Gulfport in an arbitration before Amy Totenberg. We usually silenced our phones, but I told Amy and the plaintiffs' lawyers I was expecting a call and would need to take it. My phone rang at 11:00, and I stepped out of the courtroom. The call was brief, and I stepped back inside and announced the news: "It's a boy."

Collins, the baby born that morning, is four months away from his fifteenth birthday as of Groundhog Day 2024, the day I typed these words. Ann Lowrey's fourth and last, Elsa Gray, turned ten in November.

"Oh, what a tangled web we weave, when first we practice to deceive."

I could have sworn those words were written by Shakespeare, but then I looked them up and discovered I was wrong. They were actually written by Scottish author Sir Walter Scott and appear in his poem "Marmion: A Tale of Flodden Field." The poem was published in 1808, nearly two centuries after the Bard of Avon "shuffled off this mortal coil." Shakespeare did write those words to describe the act of dying.

Scott's lines about the tangled web are famous, but they're not that easy to say. Try to do it three times real fast, and you'll see what I mean. They're right up there with the peck of pickled peppers Peter Piper picked, of which John Harris wrote in 1813. Having just learned that Scott wove his web and Harris picked his peppers only five years apart, I now dub the early nineteenth century the Golden Age of Tongue Twisters.

For obvious reasons, I chose never to use a tongue twister in an opening statement or closing argument. The same can't be said for one of the plaintiffs' lawyers, who chose to invoke the tangled web in an arbitration.

It did not go well, at least according to Davis and Adam, the two ETW members who witnessed it. The lawyer used Scott's words not only in his opening and closing but as the theme of his case. He quoted them repeatedly. Or, I should say, he tried to quote them repeatedly.

His most common mistake, per Adam and Davis, was transposing two words. The deceiver in his telling didn't weave a tangled web but instead webbed a tangled weave. When he avoided that mistake and made it through the first line unscathed, he whiffed on the second. When he tangled the tangled web for the fourth or fifth time in a row, Adam could no longer contain himself. He tried to suppress a laugh, and it came out as something between a wheeze and a chortle. Davis, who is so proper he once wore two left dress shoes to keep from having to wear sneakers (see MATCHING SHOES MATTER), gave Adam the stink eye.

All Cases Must End

After the last of the arbitrations ended, we turned our focus to the fourteen opt-out plaintiffs, whose cases had been on hold for two years. We no longer needed the entire ETW team, and responsibility for the remaining cases fell mostly to Adam and me. We settled three of them, two for nuisance value and one with significant exposure in the mid-five figures. As the months rolled by, we wrote briefs in support of our summary judgment motions in the remaining eleven and waited for rulings. If the motions weren't granted, we would finally have our first jury trials.

By early 2010, I had too little work to do for the first time in many years, but that was a good thing because I was busy with other things. My divorce from Betsy Ann was finalized during the arbitrations, just a month before a deer entered the Jollys' home without knocking. I then embarked on two serious relationships—not simultaneously, I promise—the second of which ended in the spring of 2010.

After the second breakup, I found myself at Ann Lowrey's home on a Saturday afternoon. I wasn't looking for advice, but that didn't stop her from giving it. She said I needed to stop jumping into serious relationships so fast. I needed to be patient, take my time, play the field. I agreed with her advice but wondered how I could follow it. I was fifty-two years old and wasn't likely to meet my soulmate while the two of us were sitting on bar stools. How was I supposed to meet age-appropriate women?

A recently divorced friend gave me two suggestions. One was to attend disease-of-the-month benefit functions, which he said single women were comfortable attending alone. The other was to visit different churches. I was doubtful and asked if he really searched for women at church. "Sure," he said, "I cruise the pews." Ann Lowrey had different advice. She declared that I should give eHarmony a try, turned on her laptop, and signed me up.

Finding a suitable photo for my eHarmony profile was a challenge. We both had hundreds of photos of my grandchildren on our iPhones but very few of me. One of my post-divorce girlfriends sent me titillating selfies while I was in Gulfport arbitrating, but I had never taken a selfie myself. Ann Lowrey finally found a photo we could use. It was two or three years old and was taken at the Mississippi State Fair with Ada Brooks sitting on my shoulders. Neither Ann Lowrey nor I noticed the wedding band on my left ring finger, the one I bought during my first week at Duke. The ring probably hurt my chances with some of the women on eHarmony. As for Carrie, she studied the photo with the ring on my finger and the child on my shoulders and wondered if I was a philandering pedophile.

In the weeks after I signed up for eHarmony, I would stroll into the office at mid-morning and power up my desktop. Before I even considered doing any legal work, I would study the profiles of all the women eHarmony had matched me with the night before. I took my time and analyzed them in detail. Adam, whose office was next to mine, said the firm should have put me on an unpaid leave of absence.

In the years since, when people have asked me about online dating, I've told them it's low risk and potentially life-changing reward. It's also highly entertaining. I was matched with a woman who said the five most important things in her life were Sex, God, Sex, God, and Sex. I never met her and didn't verify the claim. I was also matched with a beautiful woman who had been recognized as the world's foremost authority on cougar-cub dating relationships. We exchanged emails, but I never met her either. We were the same age, so maybe I was too old.

When I fired up my desktop on the morning of May 8, 2010, I was greeted by my life-changing reward. The night before, eHarmony had matched Carrie and me. I could see that she was beautiful from her photo and could tell that she was smart and funny from her profile, which she wrote while having wine with friends. Her profile said she saved turtles from the middle of the road when practical, loved to read, and was nearly six feet tall in heels but worth the climb. I emailed her immediately and told her I had saved many a turtle, wanted to meet her, and would bring a book and a ladder.

We began emailing constantly, then talking constantly, then dating constantly. In September I proposed, and like Delta Pine, she said yes. I still wasn't patient, but this time I was right. Unlike Delta Pine and Monsanto, there was no breakup. We planned to marry in December when my son Paul returned from a semester abroad in Scotland, but we wound up waiting till New Year's Day, 1/1/11. Why? Because my accountant said we could save enough in taxes to pay for our honeymoon if we waited until 2011 to tie the knot. I'm cheap, and it was an easy call. As for having our anniversary on New Year's Day, it's not hard to remember, but it's hard to find a restaurant.

Enough of that digression into my personal life. Now back to the remaining opt-out cases. Adam and I believed we had strong summary judgment arguments in the eleven we didn't settle, but we doubted we would win them all. Judges are human too, and we figured human nature would work against us. All the cases were weak, but we suspected Judge Ozerden would deny our motions in the least weak among them.

But the rulings trickled in, one at a time, and we kept winning. The streak continued into 2011. In March Judge Ozerden granted our motion in the case of the plaintiff who cried when he lied in an arbitration. On August 29, the sixth anniversary of Hurricane Katrina, the judge awarded summary judgment in another case. He granted the last of our eleven motions in November. The plaintiff in that case tried to appeal but missed the deadline, and the court denied her motion to extend it in May 2012. There were no more appeals and nothing left to be done. The IWFJ litigation, at long last, was over.

Jarndyce and Jarndyce, an interminable dispute over a large inheritance, plays a key role in *Bleak House*, Charles Dickens' famous novel. The case drags on for generations and comes to a merciful end only after legal fees exhaust the entire estate and there is nothing left to fight over. In Dickens' words, "The little plaintiff or defendant, who was promised a new rocking-horse when *Jarndyce and Jarndyce* should be settled, has grown up, possessed himself of a real horse, and trotted away into another world."

The real IWFJ cases did not last as long as Dickens' fictional one, and when they finally ended, I had not yet trotted away into another world or shuffled off this mortal coil. But the litigation was still the longest of my career, lasting more than eleven years. In the first ten, I changed law firms twice and residences three times, divorced and remarried, and three of my grandchildren were born, the third coming into the world one morning while I was arbitrating in Gulfport.

In the last year of the IWFJ litigation, a week after we won a case on the anniversary of Katrina, my father came to live with us. It was Carrie's idea. She is kind and generous as well as beautiful, smart, and funny. Two months later, in the month when we won the last remaining IWFJ case, we took Daddy home to Tupelo for a party to celebrate his ninetieth birthday. It was Carrie's idea. She is thoughtful too. Two months after that, we took Daddy with us to dinner on a special occasion. We went to a lousy restaurant. It was our first anniversary, and no good ones were open. Having Daddy join us was Carrie's idea. She is considerate too.

ETW Diaspora

The members of the ETW team began to scatter to the four winds even before the IWFJ cases ended. When Ann Lowrey left Baker Donelson in the fall of 2008, she was the first ETW team member to leave the firm. She taught at a preschool until Collins was born in the summer of 2009. With three children five and under, she was a stay-at-home mom for a while, then began teaching at a school designed to augment home-schooling. She was later asked by a group of parents to start a new school. She was still in her twenties, but with help from her husband, Paul, and others, she founded St. Augustine School, a classical Christian school in a Jackson suburb. The school began with fifty students a decade ago and now has more than 300. I am, you won't be surprised to learn, a proud father.

Amy and Brandon left the team and the firm after the arbitrations ended but before we received the last of the summary judgment rulings. Amy departed shortly before her first child was born. She says that giving birth and leaving the ETW team were equally painful. She later worked for several years with Ann Lowrey at St. Augustine School and is now a part-time paralegal at another Jackson firm.

Brandon grew up in Houston—Mississippi, not Texas—forty miles north of Starkville, home of Mississippi State. He went to undergraduate school at MSU and is a devoted Bulldog sports fan. In 2011 he received an offer he couldn't refuse—to join the Office of the General Counsel at his alma mater. He is now Deputy General Counsel.

Ceejaye became pregnant before the arbitrations ended. When she found out she was expecting a girl, Adam and I dubbed the baby Lurleen. Ceejaye and her husband wisely christened her Anna Mitchell instead. When their second daughter was born two years later, Ceejaye decided she needed a job with a more predictable schedule and accepted an in-house position with the largest construction company in Mississippi. Eight years after that, in March 2021, I met Ceejaye for lunch one day. I was shocked to see, just as she was shocked to learn seven months earlier, that she was pregnant again. The third Peters daughter was born two weeks later.

Davis left Baker Donelson for Butler Snow in 2018, and Adam and I left for Watkins & Eager two years after that. There were eight members of the ETW team at Baker Donelson, but Scott is the only one who still works there. He's served as the managing shareholder of the Jackson office and on the firm's board of directors. Now that Amy no longer works at St. Augustine and I no longer work at all, no members of the ETW team work together. Sad.

But at least for a few years, we had a good team, and we had a good time. To quote Texas singer-songwriter Hayes Carll, "It was good while it lasted, but it didn't last too long."

Baby Face

As noted earlier, I had a baby face when I was a young adult and looked much younger than my years. Betsy Ann did too. If you saw our wedding pictures, you would think it was an arranged marriage between two twelve-year-olds. In the decades that followed, people were often surprised when they learned my age. Sadly, that doesn't seem to happen much anymore.

In the late 1990s, I lived in northeast Jackson, a fifteen-minute drive from the office. At the end of most days, I would stop at a convenience store and buy one beer for the drive home. My standard was a twenty-four-ouncer, a so-called fencepost. It was the equivalent of two beers, but it came in one can, so I counted it as one beer.

On April 10, 1996, three months before my thirty-ninth birthday, I worked late and stopped at the Shell station on High Street for my customary fencepost. I know I stopped there that evening because of what happened when I put the beer on the counter. The cashier looked at me, then asked to see my ID. She studied my driver's license, looked at me again, then said something that was music to my ears. She couldn't believe I was that old, she told me. She said she checked IDs only for customers who looked younger than twenty-one.

I had been exhausted, but I was now both energized and elated. And I sprang into action. I told her I was a lawyer and this was important. I needed to take a statement. Having no legal pad and necessity being the mother of invention, I asked her for a paper bag. I borrowed her pen and wrote one sentence on the bag with a signature line under it. The statement I asked her to sign stated in its entirety, "I checked Brooks Eason's ID on April 10, 1996, because I thought he looked younger than twenty-one."

I then spun the bag around, pushed it across the counter, and asked her to read it carefully. If it was accurate, I said, I wanted her to sign it. She was having as much fun as I was and took her time. She then signed it, J. Anderson, and handed it back.

I was about to leave with my two treasures—the fencepost and the paper-bag statement—when my new friend asked me to give the bag back to her. She didn't recant but instead added a detail to lend further authenticity to the evidence. Across the top of the paper bag she wrote one word, "Shell," then handed it back. I still have it.

More than a decade later, after Betsy Ann and I split up but before I met Carrie, I went to see the Pates at a local watering hole on a Sunday afternoon. After they finished playing, I asked the waitress for my check, then walked to the men's room. Upon my return, I discovered a pleasant surprise. While I was gone, a very young, very attractive woman had climbed atop the bar stool next to mine. In short order, I learned that she was also very drunk and very flirtatious. Blinded by beer goggles, she was chatting me up and digging my scene.

When the waitress arrived and handed me the check, I pulled out my wallet, opened it, and revealed a picture inside. It was a picture of a baby. The drunk girl pointed to the photo and asked me who it was. Doing the honorable thing, I told her the truth. I said the baby was my granddaughter. Ada Brooks was the same age in the photo as she was in my eHarmony profile picture.

The girl stared down at the photo, then looked up at me. I wasn't supposed to be old enough to have a granddaughter. Like the woman at the Shell station, she seemed perplexed. When she looked back down at the photo, I could see the wheels turning. Despite her inebriation, and in just a few seconds, she processed the revelation, evaluated the situation, and came up with a new plan. When she looked up again, she was smiling. "You need to meet my mama," she said.

Never Mind

During the 2012 campaign, singer-songwriter James Taylor contacted President Obama's campaign officials and told them he was clearing his calendar for the last few months before Election Day. He would do what they wanted, entertain donors, whatever. Their wish was his command.

Mike Egan was one of my fellow summer clerks at King & Spalding in 1981. He's a fine lawyer and a great guy. He spent many years as a partner at K&S before going to work as general counsel and dispenser of wisdom to Arthur Blank, the co-founder of Home Depot and owner of the Atlanta Falcons, the Atlanta United soccer team, and various other businesses. Like James Taylor, Mike and his wife Mindy are Democrats. They have given generously to Democratic candidates and the Democratic National Committee.

Carrie and I host house concerts. We've had nearly fifty since we started in 2015. The concerts are wonderful. Having talented recording artists play in our living room for us and our friends is the most fun we have when we're not horizontal.

Carrie and I met Mike and Mindy for dinner when they came through Jackson several years ago. I hadn't seen them in many years, and Carrie had never met them. While we were catching up, I told them about our house concerts. I said how great they were and bragged about all the wonderful artists we'd hosted.

A good lawyer doesn't ask a question when he doesn't know the answer, at least not at trial. But I was having dinner as a friend, not a lawyer, and I asked Mike and Mindy one.

"Y'all ever been to a house concert?"

"No," Mike said, "we've never done anything like that."

Mindy corrected him. "Well, there was that one with James Taylor."

I changed the subject.

Amateur Diagnosis

I'm two years and ten days older than my friend Carter Thompson. He and I clerked together at Butler Snow in the summer of 1982. I had graduated from law school and was about to start my year with Judge Clark, and he had just finished his first year of law school at Ole Miss. He joined Butler Snow when he graduated, and we rarely saw each other for the next quarter century. But then, like Delta Pine and Monsanto and Judy and Tom, we reunited, and it felt so good. Within a span of a few months in 2007, I left McGlinchey, he left Butler Snow, and we both joined Baker Donelson. Carter's wife, Wendy, a tax lawyer, joined the firm when we did.

Carter is a big guy with an even bigger voice. He has a booming baritone and is the loudest person I know. If he weren't a litigator, he could be a disc jockey or a play-by-play announcer. He wouldn't even need a microphone.

Someone who's lacking in the looks department is often described as having a face made for radio. Carter has a voice made for radio. Also, Carter preferred, and I guess still prefers, to talk on the speaker phone. His office at Baker Donelson was two doors down from mine. Like it or not, I knew all about his cases.

Carter was on a long conference call one morning, on the speaker phone as usual, and he seemed even louder than usual. How was that even possible? My door was closed, his door was closed, but I could hear his every word. Without waiting for the call to end, I typed a short email. I addressed it to Wendy, but I copied Carter. I'm a lawyer, or at least I was then, but I offered medical advice. I wrote: "Please make Carter an appointment with an audiologist. Nobody could be that loud without being deaf." Seconds after I hit send, from two doors down, came Carter's booming laugh.

But it is my Head

Carrie and I love our house concerts, and our home is our favorite local live music venue. Our second favorite is Duling Hall, a converted elementary-school auditorium in Jackson's Fondren neighborhood. Carrie and I went there for a show by Texas singer-songwriter Robert Earl Keen in January 2016, but we didn't hear him sing a single song.

As we stood listening to the opening act, I noticed something wrong with my left arm. There was no pain, and it wasn't numb, but it felt like a dead weight hanging from my shoulder, like it needed a place to rest. I walked over to the bar and rested it there.

Between acts, Carrie asked me to describe my symptoms to our friend Ashley Seawright, an accomplished nurse practitioner. Ashley said it sounded like a stroke or a heart attack and instructed us to go straight to the emergency room at the University of Mississippi Medical Center, the same hospital where I'd refused treatment when I wrecked my VW Beetle three decades earlier. I'll let you decide if I should have refused treatment again. Ashley would call ahead, and they would be waiting. I protested—Robert is one of my favorites—but I was no match for the wife and expert. As we walked to the car, I heard the roar of the crowd as Robert took the stage.

Two nurses greeted us at the entrance to the ER, directed me to a bed, and began examining me. It seemed like much ado about very little. My speech and vision were fine, and unlike the aftermath of my wreck in 1986, I answered all the questions correctly. It was just my arm.

Soon an orderly came with a wheelchair, rolled me out for a CAT scan, then brought me back to wait for the results. A young doctor from Egypt appeared with the verdict minutes later. His name was Kareem, but he was no taller than I am. He declared that I'd had a stroke. I told him I felt fine and asked if he was sure. He was positive and said it happened several hours earlier. I told him we were leaving on vacation the next day, flying to Ft. Lauderdale for a live music cruise. It was paid for and non-refundable. I was cheap, and I felt okay. Kareem smiled, shook his head, and said I would be staying with them for a few days.

I was soon moved to a private room, where I was awakened during the night and wheeled out for another test, this time an MRI. It was my first of four, which was four too many from my claustrophobic perspective. My symptoms were worse by morning. My left hand was uncoordinated, and the left side of my face felt strange. I poked myself in the eye washing my hair and bit the inside of my lip eating breakfast.

While Carrie was at home changing clothes and getting some things for me, the head of the neurology department came in to tell me about the MRI results. He spoke with a thick German accent and had some kind of computer to show me the slides. A young man and woman, presumably med students or residents, stood beside him. They looked solemn.

He began by saying I'd had four strokes. He showed me four slides of my brain with tiny spots, each of which he said was a stroke, and identified the one that was causing my symptoms. Before showing me the next slide, he paused and said, "But of greater concern is this."

After that intro, he displayed the fifth slide, which revealed some sort of abnormality that appeared to cover nearly a fourth of my brain. When I asked what it was, his bedside manner was downright Germanic. "In all likelihood," he said, "it is either an infection or cancer. Cancer is much more common, and you have no sign of infection." I let the news sink in, then asked what was next. He said they would perform several tests to reach a definitive diagnosis. His assistants would explain the details. With that, he was gone.

I am stoic, or at least I try to be, and I listened calmly as they described the tests. Carrie returned soon after they left, and I shared the news. So I wouldn't see her, she went down to the parking lot, sat in the car by herself, and cried.

But it turned out the doctor was wrong. They did all the tests, including two more MRIs, another CAT scan, a spinal tap, and other unpleasant procedures I've blocked from my memory. They found no sign of cancer and decided a tumor was unlikely, though they still couldn't rule it out. Most brain tumors, I was told, metastasize from elsewhere in the body, but they said I looked great from the neck down. It was just my brain. "I had to pay you for that?" I asked.

When I was discharged, my hand and face were improving, but I still had the large, mysterious spot on my brain. They had no idea what it was and scheduled yet another MRI in several weeks to check it again. If the spot shrunk in the interim, that would be good. If it was unchanged, they would schedule another MRI. If it grew, they would drill a hole in my skull and do a biopsy.

Not long after my discharge, I had a follow-up appointment with a different doctor, this one from Venezuela. I was feeling fine and wanted to attend the upcoming Regression, the golf trip with my law school buddies. Carrie had read that flying not long after a stroke can be dangerous, but how long after was a matter on which neurologists disagreed. I told the doctor about the trip, and he explained the risks and offered his assessment. "You will probably be fine," he said. He then added a caveat: "But remember," he said, "it's not my head." I'm not sure what to call that kind of bedside manner. As for the Regression, I stayed home.

Several days after my fourth MRI, Carrie and I went to a place no one ever wants to go, the hospital's department of neurological oncology, to find out the results. I was still stoic; Carrie was still nervous. We were greeted by yet another doctor, one we hadn't seen before. He was an American, my first, and a little Hobbit-like guy. His lab coat was covered with stains, and his hair looked like Kramer's on *Seinfeld*. He reported that the MRI showed improvement. Carrie squeezed my leg and asked what that meant. The spot, he said, was gone. When I asked him what it was, he said he didn't know and there was no way to find out now. After all, he repeated, it was gone. I was released from the hospital's care, and my future appointments were cancelled. The spot that was there on one MRI and gone the next remains a mystery eight years later.

My hand and face were soon back to normal, and I was hiking in the mountains of Colorado by Labor Day. I was back to my pre-stroke condition physically, but the experience had changed my outlook on life. During the weeks when my future was still in doubt, I had time to think about how much time I had left and what I wanted to do with it. I made two resolutions. They were both about books, but one was far more significant than the other.

The less important one was about reading them. It so happened that I was in the middle of reading a lousy book when I had the stroke. When Carrie brought it to the hospital minutes after I learned I probably had a brain tumor, I stared at the cover, then put it down. I had finished nearly every book I'd ever started. It was a matter of self-discipline. But if I had brain cancer, I decided, I wasn't going to waste my time reading a boring book. Though it turned out I didn't have a tumor, I've maintained the practice since then.

Amor Towles, author of the magnificent novel *A Gentleman in Moscow*, gave me some advice on the subject, which he said a famous librarian had given him. Famous librarian struck me as an oxymoron, but her advice was sound. Her view was that a reader should give every book a hundred pages less his age before giving up on it. If the reader doesn't like the book by the prescribed number of pages—thirty-four pages for me at the age when I typed this—he should feel no guilt about putting it down and starting another one.

That the number of pages shrinks as the reader grows older makes sense for two reasons. As a reader ages, he should become more discerning. He shouldn't need to read as many pages as he did in his youth to decide if he likes a book. Older readers also have less time left to live and thus less time to waste on bad books.

The second resolution, which was much more important, was about writing books. Whatever my future held, I decided I wanted to spend less of it practicing law and more of it doing things that were fun and stress-free, including writing. To make that possible, I worked out an arrangement with Baker Donelson to work less and make less. I voluntarily gave up my status as an equity shareholder and agreed to a billable-hour expectation that was much lower than the norm. It was liberating. When I joined Watkins & Eager, I had no billable-hour expectation at all. If I worked, I got paid. If I didn't, I didn't. It was even more liberating. In the fifty-eight years before my stroke, I wrote one book. In the seven years between my stroke and my retirement, I wrote four.

Matching Shoes Matter

I started my career with shoes that didn't fit and ended it with shoes that didn't match. When I reached the age when men dribble food on their shirts, I wore mismatched shoes to the office one day. The shoes looked similar—they were both light brown loafers—but they sounded very different. My left shoe had a hard sole and made a distinct clicking sound on the tile floor at the office. My right one had a soft sole and made no sound at all. And yet, inexplicably, I went all day without noticing. I'd like to blame my stroke, but I suspect it was the same trait that explains my speaking to voicemails and searching for my iPhone while talking on it.

I still worked at Baker Donelson then, where two of the most valuable perks were a bar and patio on the top floor. A group of us gathered there regularly after work to have a cocktail or two and solve the world's problems. On the day in question, I mixed myself a drink and, being an outdoor guy, went out to the patio. When I pulled up a chair, I looked down and saw my mismatched shoes.

I learned from my wonderful father that being willing to make fun of yourself is an admirable trait, and I displayed my mismatched shoes to everyone I saw who was still at the office. I learned in the process that one of our colleagues, Davis "Ronnie" Frye, had once worn shoes that matched too well. I decided to talk to Davis to get the story straight from the horse's mouth. Our conversation went something like this:

Me: I heard you wore two left shoes to a mediation.

Him: It's true. I did. It was in Atlanta.

Me: How'd it happen?

Him: I had bought an extra pair of black dress shoes. You know, just in case.

Me: Very prudent.

Him: I packed in a hurry for my flight. When I was getting dressed the next morning, I discovered I'd brought the left shoe from both pairs.

Me: Bummer.

Him: You're telling me.

Me: What'd you do?

Him: I put them on.

Me: Didn't they hurt your feet?

Him: Just my right one.

Me: Why didn't you wear the shoes you wore on the plane?

Him: They were sneakers. I couldn't wear them with a suit.

Me: I would have. Did you at least take the right one off when you got to the mediation? I would have.

Him: No, I left it on.

Me: But wasn't it still hurting?

Him: It got numb after a while.

Me: What did they say when you told them about your shoes?

Him: I didn't tell them.

Me: I would have.

Him: Well, I didn't. And I don't think anybody noticed. Nobody said anything.

Me: What would they have said?

Him: Good point.

Me: Did you at least settle the case?

Him: We did. The client was very pleased.

I decided the two footwear foul-ups warranted an office-wide email. After describing what Davis and I had done, I invented a whispered exchange between the plaintiff and her daughter at Davis's mediation. It went something like this:

Daughter: Mama, look at that poor man! Look at his feet!

Plaintiff: What poor man?

Daughter: That Frye guy. He's got two left feet!

Plaintiff: What on Earth are you talking about?

Daughter: Look under the table, Mama!

Plaintiff: Lord have mercy! I've never seen such a thing!

Daughter: Me neither. That poor man. Just think what he must spend on shoes.

Plaintiff: Spend on shoes?

Daughter: Sure. You can't buy two left shoes. He's got to buy two pairs and throw the right ones away.

Plaintiff: Throw them away?

Daughter: Sure. What would he do with two right shoes? He can't even wear one of them. Poor man. Take his next offer, Mama.

Plaintiff: Okay, Sweetie. I'm ready to get this over with anyway. I'm sick of having to wear this neck brace.

A few hours after I sent the email, a woman at the firm giggled when she saw me coming down the hall. She made a confession I think I would have kept to myself. She told me she'd gotten so tickled reading about Davis's two left feet that she wet her pants. That wasn't my goal, but I counted it as a win.

Ⅰ'm nearly a decade older than Keith Ball and recruited him when I was at Brunini and he was in law school. He clerked at the firm for two summers, and we became good friends. Late one night, when I was sitting alone in our living room enjoying the quiet after putting the children to bed, I was startled by a sound behind me. Someone was tapping on the window. At this hour, who could it be? I turned and saw Keith's grinning mug. He was in the neighborhood, saw the lights on, and decided to stop for a beer and a visit. Typical Keith.

But though we offered Keith a permanent job and I put the hard sell on him, he chose another firm when he graduated. In the years that followed, our paths rarely crossed. I was busy practicing law and raising three children, and he was busy practicing law and raising twice that many. It's true; Keith and his wife, Camille, have six children. Feel free to draw your own conclusions about their sanity.

After two decades in private practice, Keith was appointed to a position as a federal magistrate judge in Jackson, and our paths crossed more often because of cases I had before him. One of his principal responsibilities was to conduct settlement conferences to get cases resolved. Like Judge Roper, he was very good at it. Unlike Judge Roper, he never yelled at me. Maybe he never had a toothache.

At the end of 2022, Adam and I had a case set for trial in federal court in Jackson. Barring unforeseen circumstances, it would be my last trial. We represented Entergy, the new name for the electric utility that had been MP&L when David Kaufman and I represented United Gas Pipe Line and Judge Roper took it out on me when it looked like our settlement was falling apart.

Shortly before the December trial date in our Entergy case, we had a settlement conference before Keith. Because I'm now writing about him in his capacity as a federal judge, maybe I should refer to him as Judge Ball. But I'm no longer an active member of the Bar, and he recently decided to leave the bench and return to private practice, so I'll stick with Keith.

I had mixed emotions about settling the case, as always. They say a tie is like kissing your sister. So is settling a case on which you've worked long and hard to prepare. I was putting together my cross-examination of the very bright plaintiff and looking forward to conducting it. On the other hand, I wasn't keen on trying a case right before Christmas, and I was tired of the stress.

Keith is very patient. I suppose raising six children will either break a man or make him patient. At several points during the ten-hour settlement conference, negotiations appeared to break down. But Keith wouldn't give up, and he wouldn't let us give up. Long after dark, when everyone else in the courthouse was long gone, we finally reached an agreement. After we went into the courtroom and put the terms on the record, it was time to go. The front door was locked, so Keith led us out the back way.

Along the way, I announced that he wasn't going to have me to kick around anymore. Adam wasn't surprised, but Keith and the plaintiff's lawyers were. Though I wouldn't get to cross-examine the plaintiff, I could live with the disappointment. My principal emotion when we walked out into the night was relief.

Epilogue

W riting a book about my life in the law has naturally made me ask myself if I miss it. The answer, like the answer to many questions, is yes and no. I miss some things about it, but there are many others I'm grateful I'll never have to deal with again.

I've written about some of what I don't miss, including the difficult people I encountered in my career. Dealing with unpleasant lawyers and those who couldn't be trusted was one of the worst things about practicing law. Lawyers have a terrible reputation. Most of the ones I dealt with were honorable, but I sure won't miss the ones who weren't.

Practicing law is grueling and labor-intensive. Nearly all of my work was by the hour. At the beginning of my career, we recorded our time in fifteen-minute increments. Clients then demanded more, and we began having to account for it by the tenth of an hour. T. S. Eliot's J. Alfred Prufrock measured out his life in coffee spoons. I grew weary of measuring mine out in six-minute increments, of being a slave to the billable hour and having to write up my time.

And then there was the stress. Stress was the single worst thing about practicing law. Litigation is extremely stressful, and I am stress prone. It was a match made somewhere other than heaven. I was always worrying about something.

The stress came from two sources. The obvious one was working in an adversary system, handling disputes for a living, and constantly facing the risk of losing. I really, really hated losing, and the older I got, the more the risk weighed on me.

The second source came from the transition of the law from a profession to a business. Lawyers now face increasing demands to be entrepreneurs as well as lawyers. It's not enough to excel at your craft. You must also market your skills to attract additional work. Those who succeed often jump ship to other firms that will pay them more. Those who don't suffer the consequences. Their compensation gets cut, and some are shown the door, "nurtured out," as the head of one of my firms euphemistically put it. The transition from profession to business has reduced loyalty in both directions. Lawyers are less loyal to their firms, and firms are less loyal to their lawyers. The change has increased the stress of a job that was already stressful enough. I understand the economic reality, but all-for-one-and-one-for-all made for a less stressful life.

That's the half-empty glass, but there are also aspects of my career that I miss. For one, I miss the opportunities to be creative. Choosing the best arguments and deciding how to make them, selecting the best strategy to set up a case for summary judgment or settlement, and picking the best witnesses to testify at trial all require thought and creativity. Good lawyers constantly ask themselves questions. If we do this, what will the other side do? If we make this argument, how will they respond? If we call this witness, what will the cross-examination look like? I enjoyed beginning a brief with a paragraph that would get the reader's attention and ending it with one that would close the sale. Don't let anyone tell you that lawyers are fungible or that litigating cases is like making widgets.

I also miss the competition. In my book about hiking trips in the West, I quoted an outdoorsman named John Murray who wrote that being in grizzly country "elevates the mountains, deepens the canyons, chills the winds, brightens the stars, darkens the forest, and quickens the pulse of all who enter it." In my experience, trying a case has a similar effect on those who enter a courtroom. It also quickens the pulse. It focuses the mind and sharpens the senses.

The competition, along with the risk of losing, can make litigation all-consuming. When I was hard at work on a case, I could have charged the client for the time I spent in the shower every morning. Once a week or so, I would turn off the water, start to step out, then turn it back on. I didn't know if I'd washed my hair, and it was better to wash it twice than not at all.

I also miss the interesting subjects I learned only because I had cases about them. I learned handwriting analysis for Baxter Brown, the science of explosions for Mississippi Chemical, and transgenic traits in crops for Delta Pine. I even learned in an Ingalls case that you can buy a vibrator with a lighted tip.

Most of all, I miss the people, both my colleagues and my clients. I miss the older lawyers who trained me and are now gone and the younger ones who worked alongside me and are now in their prime. I was honored to work with men and women who were talented and able but, more important than that, were good and decent, honest and reliable, kind and amusing. I had many good times with them, and I've enjoyed writing about them. I'm sure there are many I've overlooked, but I should mention secretaries Wessie Sims and Melissa Prewitt as well as paralegal Ashlee Hardy, the tiny dynamo who kept me organized during the last decade of my career. I also miss the many excellent lawyers I litigated against. It was a pleasure and challenge to match wits with them.

What else do I miss? Well, the paychecks were nice. I never made what partners in big firms in big cities make, but I did alright. Writing books is much more fun than practicing law, but it's far less lucrative, at least so far. Thank you for reading this one and helping make it a tad more lucrative.

I also miss the stories, and there were stories everywhere. To quote the late, great Yogi Berra, "you can observe a lot by just watching." I need to stop writing and revising this book soon to keep from having to add new stories that occur to me. The day before I wrote this paragraph, I was reminded of one when I ran into a former colleague, the one I called Tommy who called me Mr. Eason, then Colonel, then Brooks.

With all those things I miss, why did I give it up? I'm just sixty-six, I fully recovered from my stroke, and I'm in good health. Many lawyers work well into their seventies, some even longer. Do I regret retiring when I did? Not for a minute, and here's why.

For one thing, if I still had to work for a living, I would be in a real pickle these days. The shipyard, believe it or not, has not been sued in an employment discrimination case since Adam and I joined Watkins & Eager in the fall of 2020. How can they have more than 10,000 employees and not a single lawsuit? What's wrong with those people? When I was spending nearly all my time on Ingalls matters, I often worried about having too many eggs in one basket. Lucky for me, the hen waited to stop laying until I was ready, willing, and able to retire.

As for the things I miss, I've tried to replace and even improve them. I still spend time with people I like, but now I avoid the ones I don't. No more Dicks for me. I didn't have that luxury when I was practicing law. Coaching mock trial is competitive but not stressful, and writing books is creative but not grueling. I haven't replaced the paychecks, but I saved a lot because I'm cheap, and I don't need a lot because I'm cheap.

And I love the freedom of being retired. I don't set the alarm, I don't worry about work on our vacations, and I can walk our dogs as far and as long as I want. Now it's not just Junior but also Teddy, whom we rescued from a highway median in late 2023 by luring him to us with chicken nuggets. He was skin and bones and terrified of people then, but now he weighs seventy pounds and yearns to be a lap dog. We've improved his life, and he's improved ours, especially Junior's. They're best friends.

So though I had a rewarding career, I'm glad it's over. My life in the law has come to an end, and now so has my book about it. But this won't be my last one. There are still stories everywhere, and I'm still observing.

Acknowledgments

I owe a debt of gratitude to many, including my publisher Mike Parker of WordCrafts Press for his faith in me and for turning my manuscripts into books; my friend Michael de Leeuw for his valuable assistance with all my books and for singing karaoke in faux Japanese; my friend Bob Fugate for his cover illustration of Trigger on the witness stand; my wife Carrie for her encouragement and eagle eye for typos; and all the friends and colleagues who appear in these stories and made my life in the law rewarding.

About the Author

Brooks Eason, as of the publication date, is pretty sure he's retired from his life in the law. He lives in Madison, Mississippi, with his wife Carrie, three rescue dogs, and a magnificent orange tabby cat named the Count. Brooks has three children and five grandchildren, only one of whom (so far) is taller than he is. In their spare time, Brooks and Carrie walk the dogs, host house concerts, and dance in the kitchen. Brooks can be found on his screened porch, at brookseason.com, and on Facebook and Instagram. *Trigger Warning* is his sixth book.

Also Available From

WORDCRAFTS PRESS

Morning Mist: Stories from the Water's Edge
   by Barbie Loflin

First Brush Your Teeth: Grief and Hope in Real Time
   by Lisa Espinoza

Geezer Stories: The Care and Feeding of Old People
   by Laura Mansfield

An Unlikely Evangelist
   by Paula K. Parker

Against Every Hope: India, Mother Teresa, and a Baby Girl
   by Bonnie Tinsley

www.wordcrafts.net

www.ingramcontent.com/pod-product-compliance
Lightning Source LLC
Chambersburg PA
CBHW051004140626
46546CB00016B/288